More Supernatural Encounters From Law Enforcement

Elliott Van Dusen

Foreword by Loyd Auerbach

Published by IngramSpark Content

www.ingramspark.com

ISBN: 978-1-9991385-4-7

Book cover design by Cody Hess and Krusher Design

Dedication

To my beautiful fiancé, Sarah Crawley. I spent many years travelling down the pathways of life before finally finding you. Our unconditional love and loyalty to one another only grows stronger with each passing day. As we continue to build this beautiful life together, I want to thank you for loving me and always being by my side. Especially while I obsessively pursue proof of an afterlife.

To my two beautiful daughters, Sofia and Meadow. You have both given me the priceless gift of fatherhood. It is a blessing to be able to watch the two of you grow up into beautiful and independent women. I will forever love you both with every ounce of my mind, body, and soul.

Acknowledgements

It would be very remiss of me not to extend a special thank you to Sarah Crawley for editing this book. Special acknowledgement is also due to Auburn White, Andrew Baird, Mary Kovacs, Kirk Hughes, Dedrick Hilton, Chuck Bergman, Harold Feiertag, and all of those who contributed stories but have your identity concealed by a pseudonym. You exemplify Paranormal Phenomena Research & Investigation's motto of bringing the truth into the light.

Table of Contents

FOREWORD

I have been directly involved in the study of psychic phenomena, experiences, and abilities (Parapsychology) since 1979. Over the years I've met hundreds, (perhaps thousands) of people who have told me about experiences we would classify as psychic or paranormal.

However, I've been interested far longer than that, even starting a Parapsychology club in my high school in Elmsford, NY, in the first half of the 1970s. During that time, I was fortunate to meet a few prominent NY area parapsychologists who shared what they had learned of people's experiences.

In college at Northwestern University, during my studies in cultural Anthropology, I was able to gear many of my own study-interests to beliefs in the supernatural and even psychic abilities. I was also fortunate to have started out as an Astronomy major under a department chair whose name has something to do with another "unexplained" topic: Dr. J. Allen Hynek, leading expert on UFOs (at the time). I even spent time volunteering at his Center for UFO Studies.

In all the time I've been interested and involved in Parapsychology (and other topics of "unexplained phenomena" earlier in my life), I've found a truism in something Hynek told us all in a lecture on UFOs my first week of college: there is a reporting artifact when it comes to unusual experiences. People often do not tell anyone else when they have an experience with the unknown, whether ghosts, premonitions, UFOs, cryptids, or any other topical area that carries with it a stigma in the Western world.

In other words, many more people since then have spoken up about having had psychic/paranormal, UFO, or other experiences with what's often referred to as the unexplained. I can confirm this from personal experience.

Over the last 40 years I've met or otherwise spoken with people all over the US, from Canada, Japan, Great Britain, and a number of other countries who have told me their psychic or otherwise paranormal experiences. The age range has been teenagers to people in their 90s. Their education levels have been all over the map, including several with multiple advanced degrees. Occupations have varied, though I can say that most have been from the corporate and legal worlds.

Most had never related their "unusual" experiences to anyone else – or so they told me – but once they learned my own background and that I take such experiences seriously, they were more than forthcoming. They even sought me out. When asked why they hadn't told anyone else (other than those who may have shared an experience at the same time), the answers were similar: "I didn't want people to think I was crazy…weird…out of my mind…hallucinating…" and so on.

In other words, the stigma attached to having these ranging experiences causes that reporting artifact that Hynek spoke of.

So many people have had psychic experiences, (a phrase which, contrary to many of the ghost hunter reality shows, does include experiences of apparitions, hauntings, and poltergeists), that one can easily say that there's little *para*normal about them. They're normal, though perhaps rare in an individual's experience.

What's really sad is to discover that separate family members or spouses or best friends each had all had their own psychic experiences at least once, (and usually more times), in their lives but were afraid to bring up the subject with the others for fear of that societal stigma.

The same goes for work groups in specific occupations. These experiences shouldn't be locked away, they should be brought into the light where people can find commonality and support. The general public often looks to experts in Parapsychology – and unfortunately to reality TV stars and those who model themselves after the rarely educated "para-celebs" – for assurances that they are not "crazy…weird…out of their minds…hallucinating" and so on. Albeit, the explanation behind the experience may indicate a mistaken conclusion.

The general public also looks to others in authority for assurances, whether doctors, researchers in other fields, psychologists, clergy, lawyers, and yes, even law enforcement. In fact, several of my more interesting cases over the years were referred to me by police in the San Francisco Bay Area where I live. I've also had interesting conversations with law enforcement officers over the years who were either curious about working with a psychic or medium on a case, or needed advice as to *how* to work with a psychic practitioner.

And, I was honored to help write a book about the history of the US and Soviet/Russian psychic spying programs – the US program (whose last project name was Star Gate), had 17 US intelligence

—

agencies task the program over and over during its 22+ year history, including the FBI. The KGB was heavily invested in the Soviet program (see *ESP Wars: East & West* by Edwin C. May, Victor Rubel, Joseph W. McMoneagle, and Loyd Auerbach).

Elliott Van Dusen has done a great service both with his first book *Supernatural Encounters* and the one you hold in your hands (or on your e-reader). That members of law enforcement have been willing to share their experiences can only support the idea that these are not all that unusual in the range of human experience. In fact, the little bits of intuition and psychic insights officers themselves have had was labeled something specific decades ago: a "Blue Sense" (although perhaps with the RCMP it should be called a "Red Sense").

I am sure you'll enjoy reading the experiences of law enforcement in this book. You may find experiences here that resonate with your own, possibly those that provide some insight from their perspectives.

Hopefully, you may even be encouraged to talk about those unusual experiences you've had in the past.

It's not a crime to have a paranormal experience!

Loyd Auerbach, MS
Director, The Office of Paranormal Investigations
President, Forever Family Foundation
Rhine Research Center Board of Directors
Adjunct Professor, Atlantic University
Instructor, Rhine Education Center

INTRODUCTION

When I wrote *Supernatural Encounters: True Paranormal Accounts from Law Enforcement*, I had no idea how much interest it would generate. At the conclusion of the epilogue, I stated that a sequel was within the realm of future possibilities. However, it was the great number of messages I had received from readers, not unlike yourself, which truly produced this sequel. Readers expressed the great excitement and enjoyment that these supernatural stories brought to them. Other law enforcement officers had contacted me and felt comfortable enough to share their supernatural encounters. Without the sincerity from my readers and the bravery from the law enforcement officers who shared their experiences, this sequel would not be possible. For that, I am extremely thankful and hope that this sequel provides you with just as much, if not more, enjoyment.

For those readers who follow my work, welcome back and thank you for purchasing this book. For any of my new readers, it is an absolute pleasure to have you join me on this ride along into the unknown. Let me introduce myself to you.

I am the Director of the Canadian Association of Parapsychological Research & Investigation operating as Paranormal

Phenomena Research & Investigation (PPRI). Established in 1997, PPRI is a non-profit organization consisting of subject matter experts in the social science discipline of parapsychology. We offer our services, free of charge, to Atlantic Canada and the New England area of the United States. PPRI is dedicated to serving the public by conducting ethical and scientific parapsychological investigations, contributing research to the scientific community, and disseminating fact based educational information.

I have been fortunate enough to have had the opportunity to study under some of the most highly respected individuals in the field of parapsychology. My formal training in parapsychology commenced in 2000 when I enrolled in two certificate programs in parapsychology at the Nova Scotia Community College. I studied under Dr. Darryll Walsh who would later become my mentor, colleague, and most importantly, friend. I completed an introduction to parapsychology course taught by Dr. Caroline Watt from the University of Edinburgh's Koestler Parapsychology Unit. In 2001, I graduated from Stratford Career Institute's parapsychology diploma program. I would eventually pursue and earn a graduate degree in parapsychology from the American International University.

I am a big proponent of continuing education, especially in the ever changing field of parapsychology. I have completed a number of parapsychological courses from the Rhine Education Center taught by parapsychologist Loyd Auerbach, Executive Director of the Rhine Research Center, John G. Kruth, and Dr. C. M. Chantal Toporow from the Society for Scientific Exploration. I have also completed the University of Ottawa's witchcraft, magic and occult traditions undergraduate course taught by Dr. Shelley Rabinovitch, and the University of Glasgow's ancient monsters undergraduate course taught by Dr. Judit Blair. Most recently, I completed the School of Parapsychology's possession and exorcism course taught by English parapsychologist Dr. Ciarán O'Keeffe.

However, parapsychology wasn't always my primary career. I earned a Bachelor of Arts degree in criminology from Saint Mary's University in Halifax, Nova Scotia before pursuing a career with the Royal Canadian Mounted Police (RCMP). I was a regular member of the RCMP for 15 years, having spent nine and half of those years investigating homicides, sex crimes and other violent crimes. I retired as a Corporal in May 2020.

Not many individuals can sustain a living in the field of

parapsychology. Most parapsychologists can be located in university psychology departments where they conduct parapsychological research off the side of their desk. Retiring from policing has allowed to me pursue my passion for parapsychology on a full-time basis.

This book is nonfiction and the events contained herein are completely true. Due to the inherent nature of policing, namely safety and security concerns along with the dysfunctional policing culture, in which I intimately understand, some of the officers wished to remain anonymous and expressed great concern surrounding their privacy and the potential for disruptive activity. Therefore, as I always have, these concerns were taken into consideration and I have respected them throughout the writing process. Some of the officers, witnesses and their organizations involved in this book have been given pseudonyms and purposely withheld, strictly for privacy reasons. I wish to advise readers that by protecting the safety and privacy of certain individuals, it has no bearing on the validity of the events or testimony of the individuals.

Just as law enforcement officers never know what call they will have to respond to next, our time has come. Are you ready? Do you have your drink of choice in hand? We are about to go on patrol together to explore more supernatural encounters from law enforcement.

DELINE UFO SIGHTING

Our first story comes from retired RCMP Corporal Kirk Hughes who was stationed in the Northwest Territories at the same time as me. In fact, I remember RCMP management flying the officers into Yellowknife for a formal debriefing the following day after this particular UFO sighting.

Cpl. Hughes was stationed in the small fly-in community of Deline (pronounced deh-li-neh), which is home to approximately 500 people of mostly Dene and Métis descent. At the time of the incident, Cpl. Hughes was a constable, however, I refer to him as Cpl. Hughes throughout the story. The RCMP detachment consists of three police officers, usually a corporal and two constables. This northern community is located 544 kilometers northwest of Yellowknife. Cpl. Hughes advised that the community used to be called Fort Franklin. It rests on the western shores of one of the largest freshwater lakes in North America – Great Bear Lake. This community is mostly pro-police with hunting and fishing remaining an important way of life for this close-knit hamlet.

The UFO sighting occurred on September 6, 2011. Cpl. Hughes recalls the sun setting around 5:00 p.m. on that particular day.

It was a rather quiet evening, eerily quiet actually, as there was minimal activity around the Northern Store. In small remote northern communities, the Northern Stores act as your one-stop shop. It is the local grocer, bank, post office, fast food restaurant, and retail store.

At approximately 9:00 p.m., Cpl. Hughes received a call from the operational communication center in Yellowknife. The dispatcher was having a hard time relaying the call for service to Cpl. Hughes. A female witness called to report a strange light hovering to the west of Deline with what appeared to be a laser beam shooting toward the ground. Cpl. Hughes chuckled as he inquired about the caller. When the dispatcher provided the complainant's name, Cpl. Hughes began feverishly making notes in his notebook. The caller was a well-known, reputable member of the community.

As he slowly peered out his window blinds, he saw a bright light hovering above the town. The bright light was indeed shooting beams of light downward. When the beam of light hit the ground, it dispersed outward. Cpl. Hughes acknowledged that what he was witnessing was highly unusual, but believed that surely, there must be a logical explanation. He advised telecommunications Yellowknife that he was leaving his residence to investigate.

As he exited his residence, the main street was becoming inundated with townsfolk pointing at the strange light in the sky. Cpl. Hughes saw the local airport operator standing in the street. "What's that light?" he shouted. The airport operator shrugged his shoulders. "There's no planes scheduled to land tonight, eh?" asked Cpl. Hughes. The airport operator shook his head no.

Transfixed on the object in the sky, Cpl. Hughes instructed the airport operator to go to the control tower and attempt to make radio contact with the object. More and more locals started to emerge from their houses to observe the object.

Cpl. Hughes radioed the Yellowknife telecommunications center and asked if they could contact the air traffic control tower in Yellowknife to inquire about whether or not there were any planes or helicopters in the vicinity. A helicopter operating in the dark that far north would be a rare sight, especially without prior knowledge of the local airport operator.

The Yellowknife dispatcher informed Cpl. Hughes that the air traffic control tower in Yellowknife had nothing flying in the Sahtu region airspace. He directed the dispatcher to contact the air traffic control tower in Edmonton, Alberta where perhaps their radar may pick up the object. Once again, the Yellowknife dispatcher reported that the skies should be clear of any aircraft.

"Perhaps the flashing lights belonged to a down aircraft?" thought Cpl. Hughes. He called dispatch again. "Can you contact Joint Rescue Co-ordination Centre Trenton and ask if they have any active emergency locator transmitters?" he asked. On the east side of the lake perched above the tree line are known rocky outcrops. If a plane was crashing against the rocky terrain, surely it would be seen from the community.

While waiting for dispatch, Cpl. Hughes went inside the modular style detachment and pulled up the weather and sky charts. After comparing the data, he was able to determine that the flashing light outside was not a planet or a bright star. There was a thunderstorm to the south, however, the flashing light emanating toward the ground wasn't lightning.

Suddenly the phone rang at the detachment. Cpl. Hughes was expecting the dispatcher to be on the other end, however, it was the local airport operator. He advised that he had repeatedly tried to communicate with the object, but that he had gotten no response. When asked if the object could be a weather balloon, the airport operator immediately said it was nothing he had ever seen before in his thirty plus years of working at the airport. The backline rang – and this time it was dispatch. Switching phones, Cpl. Hughes was advised by dispatch that North American Aerospace Defense Command (NORAD) would be in touch with him shortly. Cpl. Hughes had come to the realization that whatever was hovering above Deline was not something easily explainable.

The few streets that exist in Deline were now alive with commotion as the locals flocked to see the bright light in the night sky. Remembering that the new detachment commander had been an air traffic controller in his previous career, Cpl. Hughes knocked on the door of the corporal's house. The corporal had just transferred to the North from a posting in British Columbia but had grown up in the North when his own father was posted there as a Mountie.

When the door flung open, Cpl. Hughes handed the corporal his binoculars. "Have you ever seen anything like that in the sky?" he asked. As Cpl. Hughes pointed to the light, the corporal's eyes peered through the binoculars. The eyes of dozens of locals were also piercing into the night sky, hoping that the RCMP would be able to give them an answer about what they were all seeing.

—

The corporal, sensing that this could be a potential practical joke on the newest member of the community, began wiping the binocular lenses with his fingers to check for any grease. However, the binoculars were clean as he continued to track the slowly bouncing light. The light had now grown brighter and began moving slightly up and down, while still sending beams of light to the ground. The corporal peered through the binoculars as Cpl. Hughes gave him the update on what had already occurred.

"Not an aircraft?" asked the corporal.

"Not one that is appearing on radar," replied Cpl. Hughes.

The noise of quads and trucks driving around the RCMP detachment gave rise to the 2nd constable, a junior police officer, who stuck his head out of the window.

"What the hell is with all the damn trucks?" said the junior constable. Both officers stopped and slowly pointed towards the light in the sky. "What the hell is that?" the junior constable barked. When both of his colleagues shrugged, the junior constable threw on his gun belt and went outside with his camera. He happened to be an amateur photographer who was excited to capture photographs of nature and the northern lights while being stationed in the North.

Armed with a professional camera and his expertise, the junior constable wanted to get closer to the object and away from the light pollution of the hamlet. Piling into the RCMP truck, all three officers drove past the airport and turned onto a dirt road leading into the barren tundra.

Meanwhile, back in the hamlet, the radio chatter was becoming frantic. Some people were superstitious, believing that the light was an omen. Others thought it was an angel, military aircraft or a drone. The locals listened eagerly to the RCMP radio, straining to catch any information relating to the mysterious light.

A short drive later, the three RCMP officers were well outside the hamlet and venturing along a vacant logging road. They eventually reached a raised vantage point overlooking the valley where the hamlet nestles onto the shoreline. The UFO had moved from its original position but continued to bounce up and down. The beam of light emanating from the object was still visible.

The junior constable snapped some photographs, as the other two officers ventured out of the truck to stare at the sky all while orientating themselves with the stars. A familiar voice crackled over the radio. It was the wife of Cpl. Hughes. Given the remote northern location, lack of resources and communication capabilities, it is not unusual to have spouses answer or monitor the radio. His wife sounded sleepy, but managed to advise that NORAD would be contacting the officers.

A call from NORAD was patched through to the police radio. The caller identified himself by name and rank and casually asked what the RCMP officers were seeing. After a brief explanation, and some co-ordinates from a map and compass, the NORAD officer said he'd call back.

An hour or so passed as the RCMP officers continued to watch the UFO. Behind them, a thunderstorm was pushing forward as the northern lights danced in the sky above. The UFO had a noticeable color tint that would occasionally change. As the three officers watched the object hover above in the night sky, the silence was broken by a radio communication.

"You guys okay?" asked Cpl. Hughes's wife.

"All good here," Cpl. Hughes responded.

"Okay, because dispatch has been trying to reach you guys for an hour and the phone and TV are down," she said.

That caught the officer's attention. After a quick press of the call button and the long-winded garbling sound of the radio, the officers were back in communication with Yellowknife dispatch. The dispatchers were concerned as the radio, fax, phone, television, and limited internet in the region had gone down, leaving the area in complete communication darkness. Cpl. Hughes responded that all was well, and that they would touch base with the satellite phone in case the radio lines went back down again.

The corporal grabbed the satellite phone hard case and opened it up. The satellite phone antenna was drawn up and the unit turned on without fanfare. The only surprise was when the satellite couldn't connect to the phone. The officers began to wonder if the object was causing some sort of interference with the satellite link.

A flicker of light caught the attention of the corporal and he began gazing upward. Cpl. Hughes also turned his attention towards the southeast part of the sky. Streaking across the horizon at subsonic speeds were two red and white lights pushing the bank of clouds ahead of them as they streaked towards the light. Radio chatter picked up, and the sudden startle of an incoming phone call broke the tension. It was NORAD.

NORAD had dispatched fighter jets to intercept the object. Cpl. Hughes confirmed that the jets were already in eyesight, but noted that the strange light was now nowhere to be seen. The three RCMP officers were stunned and stared blankly at the night sky as a light rain began to fall.

It was a painstakingly slow drive back to the detachment. All three RCMP officers shared their theories on what they had witnessed. Some of the townsfolk met the officers outside of the detachment and began asking them what the red and white lights were. Cpl. Hughes explained that they were government aircraft. The locals peered back toward the black empty sky and asked about the object. Cpl. Hughes shrugged.

"Not a downed airplane," he calmly advised, as he continued climbing the stairs to the office.

The following morning was spent taking phone calls from Yellowknife RCMP headquarters, the media and cross-referencing data in a vain attempt to label the incident. As the weeks went on, follow up phone calls were received from NORAD. The Canadian Security Intelligence Service (CSIS) sent an agent to investigate. Multiple inquiries were received from Ufologists all across North

America. Despite the amount of effort that went into investigating this sighting, the Deline UFO remains unexplained to this day.

NOT MY SON

Cpl. Bruce Edwards, of the RCMP, was posted to the western Arctic from 1997-2001. He was posted to a small hamlet of approximately 450 people located in Northern Canada. RCMP officers and their families who are posted to the Arctic are provided with government accommodations. Cpl. Edwards resided with his wife and two sons in one of these government houses. The government accommodations consisted of a double wide trailer which was divided into living quarters and the RCMP Detachment. It was here that he would have an encounter with the supernatural.

One evening, while the Edwards family slept, the sound of footsteps awoke Cpl. Edwards. The footsteps could be heard walking in the hallway coming toward the master bedroom entry way. It was early morning and the master bedroom was dimly lit from the rising sun. As Cpl. Edwards looked toward the door frame, he saw whom he believed to be his two year-old son standing there. Cpl. Edwards asked him if everything was alright, but there was no response. Cpl. Edwards then proceeded to tell his son to come here. The boy came within five feet of the bed. "Come on, hop in bed," said Cpl. Edwards. Instead, the little boy slowly turned around and began walking across the hallway into the other bedroom.

Cpl. Edwards jumped out of bed to go see if everything was alright with his son. To his astonishment, he found his son sound asleep and nestled safely in bed. Cpl. Edwards checked the rest of the house, but everything appeared to be in order.

The following day, he told his wife what had happened. His wife disclosed to him that there had been a couple of times while she was nursing their six month old son, when she began feeling like something was watching her in the nursey. Cpl. Edwards tried to convince himself that what he had witnessed was simply a dream, however, he knew deep down that he had not been dreaming. When Cpl. Edwards had transferred to this community, he was warned of a tragedy which had recently occurred on the RCMP property. He hadn't given it much thought after he initially heard the story, but his experience certainly changed that.

Approximately one month prior to his arrival, a boy not much older than Cpl. Edwards' two year-old son, had been killed near the vicinity of the property. The young boy was playing his yard on his bicycle when a service truck arrived. As the driver was backing the truck into the yard, he didn't see the boy playing. As a result, he accidentally backed up over the little boy, resulting in his instantaneous death. The RCMP investigation confirmed that it truly was an unfortunate accident.

Cpl. Edwards only saw the apparition of the little boy on that one occasion. When asked about the history of the double wide trailer, Cpl. Edwards said that it had come from a defunct town and had operated as the RCMP Detachment and living quarters. After the town dissolved, the double wide trailer was moved to the hamlet to replace its aging detachment. Cpl. Edwards also mentioned that a graveyard was situated behind the RCMP detachment and accommodations.

Unlike the locals who are born and raised in these remote Northern communities, RCMP officers only live there for two to three years before being transferred to a new location. Building rapport with members of the community is vital. It is far too difficult to learn all of the historical knowledge of a community in such a short amount of time. Cpl. Edwards spoke to one of the detachment cell guards who had been born and raised in the community. She told Cpl. Edwards that the hamlet is home to a lot of strange occurrences, and decided to share her experiences with him.

The cell guard lived just outside the RCMP compound near

the graveyard. She told Cpl. Edwards that she and her husband would hear a small child crying in their backyard. Every time they would go outside to offer assistance, there was never anybody there. These incidents had been happening prior to the little boy being killed.

The cell guard told Cpl. Edwards that on another occasion, she and her husband heard a loud crash during the middle of the night. They got out of bed to investigate and when they went into their spare bedroom, they found a big heavy book lying on the floor wide open. She and her husband couldn't figure out how the book had landed in the position it had been found in.

It seems as though this Arctic community has its fair share of supernatural activity. To this day, Cpl. Edwards still wonders about the apparition he once saw. Was it the spirit of the little boy who had been accidentally killed, or was it some other lost soul from the adjacent graveyard? The mystery remains.

UP TABLE

Cpl. Bruce Edwards was excited to share a second supernatural story with us. His sister Raylene and her friends loved to play a game called "Up Table" in a small town located in Cape Breton, Nova Scotia. Unlike the Ouija board where participants place their fingertips on a small triangular piece called the planchette, in Up Table, the participants sit at a small table with their fingertips resting upon it. They then begin to chant "Up Table" in hopes of establishing communication with a spirit. If communication is established, the table will begin to rise from its resting place. Participants can ask questions of the spirit in which the table will begin to rock backwards on two legs. Banging noises or raps are created by the spirit when responding to yes or no questions.

One summer, Raylene who was a school teacher had invited two other teachers over to her residence to play Up Table. They had the lights turned down low to create the stereotypical séance ambiance. As Raylene and her two friends continued to play Up Table, they noticed in the corner of the room some strange sparkling white lights which had materialized. Thinking it was a spirit, the three women asked the lights to leave, but the lights remained. The lights began to move from the corner of the room. Unnerved, the three women left the basement. They later went back downstairs to check and see if the lights were still there, however, they had disappeared.

Shortly after that incident, Raylene began experiencing strange occurrences in her home. On one particular evening, the family arrived home to discover a heavy book lying on the floor, open, with a porcelain doll sitting on top of it. The porcelain doll normally rests on top of a large book case located in the bedroom of Raylene's daughter.

Another time, Raylene came home to find some of her wooden block letters which normally spell the word "B-E-L-I-E-V-E" to be reversed. The letters had been sitting atop their downstairs mantel. Her daughter wasn't living at home during this time, so she suspected that her husband Colin had changed the letters around. When she questioned him, however, Colin denied culpability.

Late at night while she was fast asleep, Raylene would feel somebody sit down on the edge of the bed. She would wake up expecting to see Colin getting into bed, however, there would be nobody there. That wasn't the only strange thing occurring during the night. On another occasion, her son was home visiting and he would sleep in the basement where Raylene and her friends would play Up Table. He woke up during the night and came upstairs to get a drink of water. As he was walking up the basement stairs, he saw an arm and hand hanging onto the railing which rounded the corner. Terrified, he turned around and ran back to the downstairs bedroom and proceeded to lock the door.

The following day, he told Raylene what had happened. She made the mistake of telling their mother, Mrs. Edwards who was a devote Catholic, what had happened. Mrs. Edwards called her local priest and convinced him to come over to bless the house and sprinkle holy water amongst the rooms.

Cpl. Edwards advised me that his sister and her two friends are some of the most normal and honest individuals one could meet. He had never questioned the validity of Raylene's story. In fact, in 2011 Cpl. Edwards and his wife were visiting his aunt in Prince Edward Island. Raylene and her husband Colin had come over for a visit as well. As they sat around their cottage telling old family stories, the topic of Up Table surfaced. Cpl. Edwards' aunt and Raylene wanted to play a game of Up Table. Cpl. Edwards wife wanted no part of it and retired to bed early. He was reluctant to play, but eventually was coaxed into it by Raylene and his aunt.

The three of them were able to make the table rock and he had no idea how they were doing it. The table was just a simple pressboard table from Ikea but it was rising approximately two feet off of the floor and would slam down hard when answering their questions. His aunt who was also a devote Catholic was so freaked out that they decided to stop playing. Cpl. Edwards remembers the table rocking like crazy at one point. Being a critical believer, he chuckled to himself and dismissed it all as just being fun and games.

However, that was the first and last time he would play Up Table. Although he is a critical believer, he prefers not to dabble in the occult and, as the old saying goes, let sleeping dogs lie.

If it wasn't a spirit communicating with Cpl. Edwards and his family, then it is possible that it was a natural and biological phenomena called the ideomotor response. Although more commonly seen with the Ouija board's planchette, ideomotor responses have also shown to affect table-turning (another name for Up Table) during séances.

WHATÍ, NORTHWEST TERRITORIES

Black chlorite stone carving of the Bushman
(Carving and photo courtesy of artist Dave Zachary http://www.davezachary.ca)

Situated on the 63rd parallel north in Canada's Northwest Territories is the small indigenous community of Whatí (pronounced wha-tee). Home to approximately 500 people, this remote hamlet is surrounded by thick woodland known as the boreal forest. Any RCMP officer posted to this community is quickly warned of the dangers which lurk in the bushes. The indigenous people call it Nàhga (pronounced na-ga), or in English, the Bush Man. This creature has been described by those who have seen it as being a hairy ape-like creature that walks upright. This Bigfoot type creature is accused of possessing magical skills used to kidnap children and bush camp workers. Folklorists have traced stories of Bigfoot as far back as medieval times in Europe. The belief is strongest in North American and Native American folklore. In *Supernatural Encounters: True Paranormal Accounts from Law Enforcement*, we heard two Nàhga accounts from Sgt. Peter Starzky. This time we hear an account from Cst. Nolan Redder of the RCMP. Cst. Redder was posted to Whatí approximately 10 years after Sgt. Starzky.

Shortly after Cst. Redder was posted to Whatí, the local townsfolk began telling him stories of Nàhga. Personally, Cst. Redder does not believe, but he reaffirmed the fact that the indigenous community of Whatí most certainly does. He recalled organizing a youth camp in which he had an Elder in the community attend for the purpose of sharing stories about their cultural past. For an hour and half, she talked about Nàhga and how the community has tried to set up protective barriers to keep Nàhga out.

One evening in the Fall of 2019, Cst. Redder and his partner received a report of a female who could be heard screaming in the woods. They began conducting neighbourhood inquiries, an age old investigative technique in which law enforcement speak with community members to gather more information about a situation.

During the inquiries, the majority of citizens Cst. Redder spoke with, stated that they distinctly heard the sound of a female screaming. The locals began telling the RCMP that they believed it was Nàhga and that he must have snatched someone from the community. Some citizens even showed Cst. Redder videos of what they claimed were the sounds of a Nàhga screaming.

As an experienced RCMP officer who grew up and worked in small isolated communities his whole life, Cst. Redder began to deduce that he could be dealing with an animal such as a fox. Female foxes are known to sound like a screaming woman or a crying baby when they are ready to mate. There was also a porcupine killed in the area at the time of the call. However, one citizen reported that he heard the female yell "Help me!" which raised a concern for Cst. Redder.

The location where the screaming occurred also concerned Cst. Redder. The wooded area had a trail which led to a large pond. Cst. Redder was concerned about the potential of someone drowning in the pond. Cst. Redder and his partner drove their police truck down the trail. While driving, they came across a fox which further supported Cst. Redder's belief that the screams may have simply been a mating call. However, the one citizen who reported that he had heard "Help me!" nagged at Cst. Redder.

Cst. Redder called Yellowknife to request Police Dog Services, however, given the time of night and remote location of the community, the police dog and his handler were not available until the following morning. Cst. Redder and his partner required more resources to assist, so they contacted the Canadian Rangers.

The Rangers are associated to, and trained by, the Canadian Army. They are often compiled of local residents who live in remote and isolated communities and can be activated to assist in public safety operations. The Rangers, Cst. Redder, and his partner began going door to door in the community to see if anyone was missing. After four hours of canvassing, everyone in the community was accounted for.

The following morning, the RCMP plane transported the police dog and his handler to Whatì. The handler worked with the police dog in an attempt to locate any sign of a missing person, but the search produced nil results. Without someone being reported as missing and exhausting all investigative avenues, Cst. Redder had no choice but to conclude his file. I asked Cst. Redder whether or not he included Nàhga in his official police report. "No, I don't want to be that guy," Cst. Redder laughed.

So many questions remain unanswered with Cst. Redder's experience. What made that horrific screaming noise in Whatí that night? Was it in fact someone in peril who has yet to be reported missing? Was it a wild animal or even Nàhga himself? One thing is for certain, Nàhga continues to terrorize the community of Whatí.

911 CALL FROM THE FUNERAL PARLOR

In 2005 on a sunny summer day, Cst. Alyssa Belanger was a fairly new police officer patrolling in Antigonish, Nova Scotia. Suddenly a call for service came across the radio. The RCMP telecommunications center in Truro had received a "static 911" call from one of the local funeral parlors.

A static 911 call is exactly as it sounds. It is when a dispatch center receives a 911 call but the dispatcher can only hear static on the other end of the line. These types of calls are common during a rain or wind storm. Police are required to attend these call as there have been some unfortunate incidents in which someone has managed to call 911 but then becomes incapacitated or unable to speak. Police cannot assume that a static 911 call was made in error.

Cst. Belanger arrived at the funeral parlor. She exited her police vehicle and began checking the premises as she was trained to do. When she knocked on the door to the funeral home, there was an employee working alone inside. Cst. Belanger recalled the employee looking like Lurch from the *Addams Family*. She said that he was very tall and friendly. He was wearing stereotypical funeral home clothing and spoke very slow and deliberate.

The employee told Cst. Belanger that he had not made a 911 call. She explained to the employee that she was legally required to check inside the funeral home in order to determine for herself that there was no emergency. The employee led Cst. Belanger to the only portable phone in the parlor which was located in the kitchen. As she scrolled through the phone, she could see that 911 had not been called from that phone line.

As Cst. Belanger began walking down the hallway of the funeral home, she felt a distinct cold wind surround her. She said it made her feel very uneasy. As she continued down the hallway, she entered the funeral home's morgue.

As the employee had indicated, there was no phone in the morgue. There was a deceased body lying on a table which had been recently prepared for burial. Cst. Belanger noticed that there was an outside phone line jack in the wall next to the body.

With no inclement weather or apparent reason for the 911 call, Cst. Belanger couldn't help but wonder to herself if dispatch had received a call from beyond the grave.

Phone calls from the dead are one of the more frequent forms of after death communication (ADC). This widely reported phenomenon usually occurs within the first 24 hours after a person's death. Recipients often report extreme difficulty in hearing the caller speak due to the sound of static. The majority of recipients report that the purpose of the ADC was to let them know that their friend or loved one passed over okay. Others have reported having a very vivid conversation with the caller, seemingly forgetting that they had died. After the phone call ends, the sudden realization that they were talking to a deceased person seems to resonate with them.

I had what some would call an ADC dream in 2006 after my father, Neil, had passed away. He had contracted Hepatitis C through the Canadian blood system and eventually succumbed to the virus at the age of 48. ADC's while sleeping often appear in dream-like states in which the experience is more vivid, colourful, and emotional than a regular dream. In my dream, he called me on a telephone to let me know that he had crossed over to the other side and that he was okay.

Although I am a believer in after death communication, I am unsure if my experience was supernatural in nature. In my circumstance, I have no way to scientifically differentiate an ADC from a dream. Either way, it was comforting nonetheless.

THE BASEMENT DWELLING GHOST

After her posting in Antigonish, Cst. Alyssa Belanger was transferred to Indian Brook for five years. She then transferred to Enfield, Nova Scotia. In 2009, Cst. Belanger was working a day shift. She and her partner had received a call from a woman who said that she was hearing some strange noises coming from her basement. The officers told her that they would be there as soon as possible.

As they arrived at the private residence, Cst. Belanger noticed a look of fear come over her partner's face.

"Oh, this house?" he said sheepishly.

"What?" said Cst. Belanger.

"Oh, nothing," he replied.

Cst. Belanger recognized that her partner was acting strange, but they had a call to attend to. The two officers knocked on the door and were invited into the house by the complainant. She had two young children with her and she was visibly shaking. She told the officers that she was very scared because she was home alone and kept hearing strange noises coming from the basement.

Cst. Belanger and her partner went downstairs to the basement. It was dark and dreary looking with no natural lighting.

—

Located in the corner of the basement was a single unused room. Both Cst. Belanger and her partner had their flashlights on and were cautiously scanning every nook and cranny. However, they found absolutely nothing. There was not even a mouse, leaving no explanation for the disruption.

They looked at each other and shrugged. Cst. Belanger and her partner turned around and began walking toward the staircase in which they descended from. What happened next was something that one would expect when watching a horror movie. Cst. Belanger said that someone or something threw a child's ball toward her and her partner. As they were approaching the stairs, they could hear the distinct sound of the plastic ball hitting the cement floor and bouncing toward them. As both officers turned around, they could see that it had come from the empty black room they had just been in.

Cst. Belanger began to run up the stairs and told her partner that he was on his own. Her partner also did not waste any time and hightailed it out of the basement. They told the home owner that they didn't find anything downstairs. Cst. Belanger was relieved for the home owner when she saw the lady's husband arrive home, just as she and her partner were departing.

As Cst. Belanger began typing her police report in the cruiser, her partner told her that he had a confession to make. He disclosed to her that when they pulled up to the house, he immediately recognized it. He further said that some of the local residents had warned him that it was a very haunted house. Cst. Belanger was never called back to that residence. She still wonders if the home owners or any other police officer ever had a supernatural encounter at that location.

ESKASONI UFO SIGHTING

Cst. Alyssa Belanger's third and final story comes from a small Cape Breton indigenous community called Eskasoni. Eskasoni is derived from the Mi'kmaq word "We'kwistoqnik" which means "where the fir trees are plentiful". The community has approximately 4,000 people.

It was March 2020 when the world had just begun shutting down in an attempt to curb the spread of COVID-19. Cst. Belanger and her partner were patrolling around Eskasoni in separate police vehicles. She noticed what can only be described as a "laser beam" shining from the night sky. She radioed her partner and he advised that he too could see it. Cst. Belanger said that the object was moving extremely fast, it wasn't anything that a human could manoeuvre.

She and her partner pulled into a parking lot and continued to observe the unidentified aerial phenomena. After seeing three bursts of the "laser beam", Cst. Belanger began rapidly blinking her flashlight at the object. Her partner was afraid and told her not provoke whatever the object was. Cst. Belanger wasn't afraid but her partner had decided that he had seen enough and chose to go back on patrol. After a few more minutes of observation, the object simply disappeared.

I checked with the UFOlogy Research of Manitoba to see if anyone else had reported any UFO sightings in Eskasoni in March of 2020. UFOlogy Research of Manitoba has been in operation since 1989. They collect and compile UFO sightings from researchers all across Canada and publish an annual report which is made available for public viewing. There had been no other UFO sightings in Eskasoni that year. However, 365 kilometers away on April 25, 2020 in Cole Harbour, Nova Scotia someone had witnessed a similar event described as "lights in a straight line like a laser moving horizontally then disappeared one at a time". The incident was reported to the Mutual UFO Network (MUFON) which investigates UFO sightings.

Cst. Belanger had mentioned that I was the first person to hear about this UFO sighting. The Eskasoni RCMP never received any calls relating to the flying object. The incident remains unexplained.

BIRDS OF A FEATHER FLOCK TOGETHER

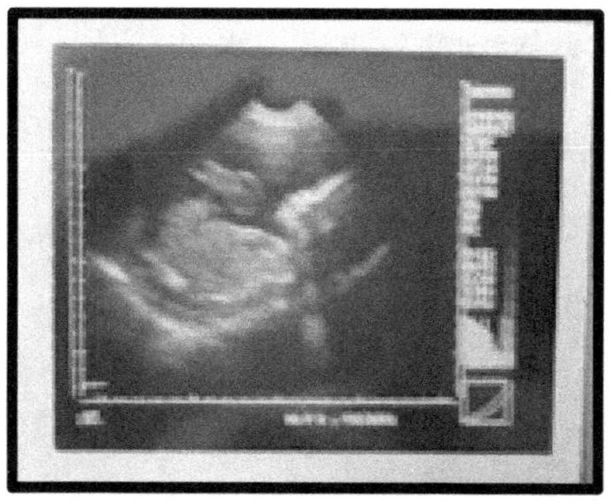

(Neveah Sarah Auld who passed away in utero and was still born on August 29, 1986.
Photo courtesy of Mary Kovacs.)

In April, 2021 I was contacted by Mary Kovacs who was willing to share her sorrowful but incredible story. Ms. Kovacs had served with the Canadian Department of National Defence for 25 years as a civilian security guard.

In 1986, she was living in Freiburg, Germany. During that time, she was seven months pregnant with a baby girl named Neveah Sarah Auld. However, on April 26, 1986 disaster struck when the Chernobyl nuclear power plant had a terrible accident. Tragically, a follow up ultrasound showed that one of Neveah's hands were deformed and looked similar to a microphone. Many unborn children succumbed to the nuclear fallout from Chernobyl. Ms. Kovacs medical team tried their very best to save Neveah, however she died in the womb and was stillborn on August 29, 1986 at 11:11 a.m.

Ever since Neveah passed away, Ms. Kovacs feels her daughter's presence which is often times confirmed by the appearance of mysterious feathers. In fact, a feather appeared by Ms. Kovacs foot before she decided to contact me with her story.

(A feather which appeared at Mary Kovacs foot before contacting Elliott Van Dusen on April 26, 2021. Photo courtesy of Mary Kovacs.)

Neveah is not the only spirit who leaves Ms. Kovacs feathers. In another tragic set of circumstances, Ms. Kovacs brother Jessie was murdered in his London, Ontario apartment in 2011 during a home invasion. Although the two men responsible for is death were apprehended and convicted, it doesn't right a wrong. After Jessie's murder, Ms. Kovacs would find larger feathers which were more distinct than the ones left by Neveah.

On July 18, 2005 Ms. Kovacs abusive relationship came to a head when her partner had her arrested during a domestic disturbance. In Canada, police officers are often times compelled to make an arrest during a domestic disturbance due to the high risk of lethality which often occurs in domestic abuse situations.

She was taken to the Elgin-Middlesex Detention Centre in London, Ontario. The cell was made entirely of concrete and measured approximately four feet long and three feet wide. Ms. Kovacs said she will never forget just how cold it was inside her cell. The detention centre has a notorious reputation for being an unfit facility. In 2013, a $325 million dollar class action lawsuit was initiated against the institution for overcrowded and unsanitary conditions, abusive and negligent correctional officers and management, and improper medical treatment for prisoners.

At 5:55 a.m., she was awake in her jail cell when a correctional officer came through the cell block and began rousing the prisoners. As he walked past each cell, he clanged a tin cup against the steel bars. He was asking if any of the prisoners wanted a cup of coffee. Ms. Kovacs sat up quickly after she felt someone touch her shoulder. It felt like a little tiny hand touching her.

After being arrested and spending the evening in such appalling conditions, she was very distressed. As she turned her head toward whatever was touching her, she saw a little hand resting upon her shoulder. She heard a voice say "You are going to be OK mom".

As she continued to turn, she saw a full apparition of whom she believed to be her daughter. She was being held by another man whom she described as looking similar to Jesus. She would later find out from her mother that the description matched that of her other, older brother who had passed away. Her brother stood silently in the jail cell smiling at her.

This experience brought Ms. Kovacs a sense of peace in what can only imaginably be a dark time in her life. Fortunately, there was a happy ending for Ms. Kovacs. The prosecution did not have any evidence to proceed to trial and the charges against her were withdrawn. She is no longer in an abusive relationship and spends her time advocating against domestic violence and promoting equal parenting rights.

I was told another story by a gentleman who seemingly had a spectral admirer. After he had his first knee replacement, the gentleman would often wake up during the middle of the night in tremendous pain. One night, he felt the end of his bed compress downward as if someone was sitting on it. Initially he thought it was his wife, but it was not. The man described seeing a female apparition with long dark brown hair wearing a light blue dress. The spirit was sitting at the end of his bed as she began rubbing his knee. Not knowing what to say or do, the man thanked the spirit. He no sooner spoke the words and as quickly as she had appeared, the female apparition suddenly stood up, walked toward the master bedroom closet, and disappeared.

Apparitions providing someone comfort during distressing times is not unheard of. In 1997, clinical parapsychologist Jim Houran and his colleague Rense Lange conducted an analysis on 49 deathbed visions. They concluded that the deathbed experiences, although fundamentally hallucinations, were comforting in nature.

RIVERVIEW HOSPITAL

(Photo courtesy of Cst. Susan Morrison.)

Situated at 2601 Lougheed Highway in Coquitlam, British Columbia stands the abandoned Riverview Hospital. This eerie but cinematic worthy location has had scenes filmed onsite for television shows such as *The X-Files* and *Supernatural*, and blockbuster movies including *The Butterfly Effect* and *Deadpool 2*.

This location is much more than a make shift Hollywood set. The Provincial Lunatic Asylum in New Westminster became overrun with admissions resulting in a new institution having to be built.

Riverview Hospital was originally named the Hospital for the Mind at Mount Coquitlam. It was first opened on April 1, 1913 and continued operations up until July 2012. Riverview Hospital, like most other psychiatric facilities of its time, has a history filled with tragedy and despair. It is a known fact that inhumane medical practices were used to treat hospital patients. In 2005, nine women received compensation for being illegally sterilized at the facility.

In 1922, the hospital incorporated a Boys Industrial School which was designed to cure delinquency through physical labour. Patients were tasked with farm chores at what was called Colony Farm. At its peak, patient labour produced 700 tonnes of crops and 20,000 gallons of milk per year.

The property also houses a hospital cemetery on the lands which was first established in 1958. There are 1,085 bodies resting in the cemetery. The majority of the bodies are patients who had no family. However, there are some staff members buried there as well. The last internment at the cemetery was the skeletal remains of a Jane Doe on April 4, 2012. Her skeleton was used at the hospital for medical instruction and other purposes.

Given its history, it is not a surprise that Riverview Hospital has been deemed one of the most haunted locations in British Columbia, Canada. The *Huffington Post* reported that an ex janitor experienced the sounds of snickering, laughing, and whispering while working alone in a decommissioned part of the building.

RCMP Cst. Susan Morrison's first posting was Coquitlam, British Columbia. The Riverview Hospital falls within the patrol area of Coquitlam detachment. When she first started working at the detachment, her trainer warned her to never attend Riverview Hospital at night because of the strange things that have occurred. Any police recruit will tell you that their trainers and co-workers can't be trusted. They love to play pranks on the rookie. I have witnessed some comical and creative schemes designed for new recruits.

One evening during the summer of 2019, the detachment received a request to respond to an alarm call at Riverview Hospital. Due to the popularity of the area, break-ins are a common occurrence. Although the hospital is not operational, the buildings are alarmed because film crews still use the building for movies and television shows. There is also a private security company hired to patrol the property. Approximately six officers responded to the call. Upon arrival, Cst. Morrison noticed an open window in which someone could have entered through. Given the size of the property, the officers decided to split up into pairs of two.

Cst. Morrison and her partner were assigned to check the basement of the one of the buildings. As soon as they made their way downstairs to the basement, Cst. Morrison's fully charged flashlight died. She looked at her partner who was a brand new recruit with only five months of service.

"Ok, we are done," Cst. Morrison said.

"But we aren't finished our clearing," he responded.

"Well, this is the start of every horror movie, we are not continuing to clear this basement," replied Cst. Morrison. When Cst. Morrison and her partner made their way back upstairs, they ran into another female officer. Coincidently, the other female officer's freshly charged flashlight had also died. Cst. Morrison's *Fenix* flashlight never worked again after that call.

It is common during supernatural encounters for electronic equipment to fail. I have personally witnessed this during many haunting investigations and once during a UFO sighting.

With respect to hauntings, it is believed that the discarnate entity draws upon the energy from batteries and electronic devices in order to produce manifestations through what is known as psychokinesis. Psychokinesis "PK" literally translates as "movement by the mind." A PK experience entails an apparent mind-over-matter effect, that is, a case where an individual's thoughts or preferences appear to have had a direct influence upon the structure of the physical environment.

Cst. Morrison and I talked about the residual energy which must remain at Riverview Hospital. Cst. Morrison said that every time she has attended the property, she can sense the negative energy. Parapsychologists believe that energy can be imprinted into the environment. Given the conditions that psychiatric patients faced during its operation, no wonder this retired hospital is a hot bed for paranormal activity.

THE ATLANTIC POLICE ACADEMY

Our next couple of encounters were experienced by Cst. Jayson Chandler. Cst. Chandler was a uniformed police officer in Pictou County, Nova Scotia during his law enforcement career. He kept weird hours and experienced notable unexplained events during the nightshift as a patrol officer.

Cst. Chandler was accepted into Holland College's Atlantic Police Academy located on beautiful Prince Edward Island. He commenced his basic training in January 2001. The first month of training can only be described as hellish. Every police officer experiences this kind of hell where the corporals or sergeants terrorize you by conducting unannounced dorm inspections during the middle of the night. It is a test to determine who has a keen sense of observation and an attention to detail. It also helps weed out those who are not cut out for the gruelling career of policing which lies ahead. After the first month, Cst. Chandler noticed that the instructors began easing up on the police cadets.

Approximately three months into his training, he and his troop experienced a very strange occurrence one evening. Everyone was sound asleep in their beds when suddenly the loud sound of military boots began pounding down the tile floors in the hallway. Whoever was walking down the hallway, were doing so with purpose. Most of the police cadets woke up in a panic and suspected that the sergeants were conducting room inspections at 4:00 a.m.

There were 14 police cadets on Cst. Chandler's floor. They all began piling out into the hallway standing at attention waiting for inspection. When Cst. Chandler exited his room, there were already four of his troopmates standing out in the hallway at attention. Cst. Chandler gave himself one final look over and then came to attention. After a few moments, 12 of the 14 police cadets were standing at attention. Two police cadets who were heavy sleepers were still sound asleep in their rooms.

Cst. Chandler was nervous for them, because he was stuck at attention and could only imagine the hell the instructors were going to put those two cadets through for not waking up and standing with their troopmates. Cst. Chandler and the other cadets didn't see any of the instructors in the hallway, but they stood at attention for approximately 10 minutes. After the 10 minutes had elapsed, some of the cadets began asking each other if they had heard the footsteps.

Cst. Chandler spoke up and said that he had heard someone

coming down the hallway with heavy boots on and they sounded like they were pissed off. The other cadets validated Cst. Chandler's experience and said that they too, had heard the exact same thing. The cadets were confused on what they should do. They knew if they went back to bed and it was an inspection, they would all pay the price. One of the cadets broke rank and went to check the sign in book at the front door, however, nobody had recently signed in. The Atlantic Police Academy strictly monitors access to and from the dormitories.

The police cadets waited at attention for another 10 minutes, but when nobody came to inspect them, they made a group executive decision to go back to bed. Everyone went back to bed and there were no further issues. The following morning during applied police sciences class, one of the cadets asked the sergeant if they did an inspection last night. The sergeant had a confused look upon his face. The cadets began explaining to the sergeant about hearing the footsteps in their dormitory at four in the morning.

The sergeant took this incident very seriously. While standing at the front of the class, he yelled out "Whoever the fuck decided to prance down the hall at four in the morning with their boots on, let me know right now!" There was silence amongst the cadets. The sergeant advised that he was going to review the security footage in the dormitory. Still, there was silence. Cst. Chandler figured if it was a prank, someone would own up to it. Any police officer who underwent basic training knows the fear a cadet feels when the troop is in trouble. In policing, one can make a major mistake and still keep their job so long as they are honest about what happened. A police officer's integrity is everything. If you are caught lying or being deceitful, your career is essentially done. Still, no one admitted to this incident being a prank.

Later that afternoon, the sergeant opened a formal investigation into the incident. One of the other instructors came into the classroom. This instructor was more gentle than the sergeant. He told the class that they are concerned about the incident. He asked the class to let him know if it was a prank, so that he could handle the situation informally. Once again, no one came forward admitting responsibility.

The incident was investigated as a break and enter investigation. The instructors checked the surveillance footage. The only camera covering the entrance and exit doors did not show anyone enter or leave the building at the time of the incident. They also checked the security card log system, however, no one had accessed the building during that time frame.

After three days into the investigation, one of the other instructors who was a polygraph operator came into Cst. Chandler's class. He told the class that they were not the first troop to report a similar incident. In all sincerity, he told the class that every two or three years, a troop will report a similar story. According to the instructor, several years previous, a cadet shot himself in the dormitory on the exact same floor Cst. Chandler's troop was being housed on. The instructor explained that this was why policy forbids cadets to keep their firearms with them until the commencement of their on the job training.

Was it the deceased cadet walking the halls? Cst. Chandler doesn't know for sure. What Cst. Chandler does know, is that 12 cadets wouldn't have mistaken the loud auditory sound of police footwear marching down the hallway. His troopmate in the room next to him said he had opened his bedroom door approximately three seconds after hearing the footsteps. When his troopmate peered out into the hallway, there was nobody there. The troopmate could still hear the distinct sound of footsteps marching down the hallway despite there being no present.

This encounter sounds like it could be a residual haunting. A residual haunting is when an apparition replays the same scene over and over again at a specific place much like a hologram or a video recording. The apparition is unaware of its surroundings and does not communicate with anyone present. Parapsychologists believe this type of haunting to be an environmental energy imprint. It is theorized that light particles are trapped and suspended in the atmosphere where they lay dormant until certain environmental factors stimulate them. These apparitions have often times met a violent and untimely death, such as the murder victim in this particular story.

THE BOXER

Cst. Chandler has always been a very factual person, especially being involved in the policing profession. He is not the type of person that sees a sheet blowing in the wind and thinks it is a ghost. It has to be something pretty inexplicable for him to classify it as supernatural. There is one experience that still haunts him to this day.

At approximately 3:00 a.m. in February 2008, Cst. Chandler and his colleagues had just finished dispersing the bar crowd. Any police officer who has worked in a community with a local bar or tavern knows the responsibilities that come with this duty. Breaking up fights, preventing property damage, extinguishing public drinking and scolding patrons who feel it necessary to urinate in the town's planters are just some of those responsibilities.

The community in which Cst. Chandler policed contained many steep hills in their roadways. It was pitch black out, but there was a fresh blanket of glistening white snow which had recently coated the roadways. He was riding in the passenger seat of the patrol vehicle when he and his partner came to the crest of a hill. He noticed a male with no shirt on, who was walking in the middle of the street approximately 600 feet in front of them. Cst. Chandler watched the big brawny gentleman air boxing by himself while standing in the middle of the roadway.

Cst. Chandler watched as the gentleman was throwing intense left hooks and right jabs. He thought to himself "Oh, here we go. A drunk we are going to have to deal with who is rowdy and likes to box." At this point, he and his partner didn't say a word to one another. Cst. Chandler would later find that that they were both thinking the exact same thing. They both reached down almost simultaneously and grabbed their Kevlar search gloves. Cst. Chandler muttered to his partner "Holy ... here we go."

As they began ascending up another hill, they momentarily lost visual sight of the male. They were travelling slower than usual due to the terrible road conditions. As they began to descend down the hill, the male had vanished. They hadn't seen him disappear. He was just simply gone.

Cst. Chandler and his partner thought that the male must have seen their police car and began running, so they picked up their pace a little bit. However, as they reached the location where the male had been, they noticed that there were no footprints in the snow.

They pulled the police vehicle over to the side of the road and proceeded to look for the male on foot. As Cst. Chandler scanned the area, he only saw footprints which had been generated by himself and his partner in the snow. "Where did the boxing male go?" wondered Cst. Chandler.

Cst. Chandler and his partner did not take this situation lightly. They were concerned for the male given his standard of dress and the inclement weather. They weren't sure if he was a trouble maker, intoxicated, or possibly experiencing a mental health crisis.

Cst. Chandler's partner was frantically trying to find the male. He was trekking through the snow filled ditches looking for some sign of recent human activity. They both jumped back into the police vehicle and turned on the alley lights. Cst. Chandler said that it was an agonizing situation, especially given the freshly fallen snow and lack of footprints. There wasn't the faintest sign that anyone else, besides the two officers, had been in that area.

Cst. Chandler and his partner finally began communicating to one another. Cst. Chandler asked his partner what he had seen. His partner said that he had seen "a large fella in the middle of the street air boxing." Cst. Chandler breathed a sigh of relief to have his observation confirmed. Cst. Chanlder told his partner that he had seen the exact same thing. They searched but were never able to find the gentleman.

The following day, Cst. Chandler and his partner had to make an occurrence report on the incident. Before writing anything, Cst. Chandler went to the Chief of Police and asked if there were ever any events in that area involving a boxer. The Chief had not heard of anything.

The only other details that Cst. Chandler could recall was that the boxing male appeared to be slightly "hazy" or "somewhat translucent" and there was a strong feeling of dread. It was a very uninviting, disturbing and sickening feeling like none other.

Had there not been fresh snow on the ground, Cst. Chandler said he would have come to the conclusion that the male had simply run away after spotting the police vehicle. However, this was not the case. Cst. Chandler also told me that if he had been by himself when the incident occurred, he would have probably chalked it up to being a sleep deprivation hallucination, especially given the late hour of the occurrence. However, mass hallucinations are an extremely rare phenomenon. For that reason, parapsychological investigators love when encounters such as this one have multiple witnesses. It gives the incident much more credibility.

This is certainly an interesting sighting reported by two credible witnesses. The boxing male was inappropriately dressed for the weather and didn't fit his environment. The male, according to Cst. Chandler, was "hazy" or "somewhat translucent" which has been reported in other apparitional sightings. It is the lack of footprints in the snow which truly peaks my curiosity about this incident. Based on what Cst. Chandler and his partner had witnessed, there should have been some sign of disturbance in the snow. The case of the boxing ghost remains a mystery.

THE ALLEYWAY GHOST

Our third supernatural encounter reported by Cst. Chandler occurred when he was working by himself. It was approximately 2:30 a.m. and he was well into his night shift. He was chatting to the local dispatcher at his police station to help break up the long nightshift. As they were talking, he noticed a male wearing a long black hooded sweatshirt approaching the little peculiar alleyway where the police officer's would park their personal vehicles. It was unusual for someone to be walking down this alleyway at 2:30 a.m.

The door to get into the alleyway was conveniently located right outside of the dispatch office. Cst. Chandler wanted to wait for the male to get closer to the door before he made the decision to challenge him. As soon as Cst. Chandler saw the male approach the door way, he snapped the door open as hard and as fast as he could. To his surprise, there was nobody there.

Cst. Chandler checked around the parked vehicles and in behind the dumpster in the unlikely event that the male was hiding, but they were both clear. The alleyway was completely undisturbed. Cst. Chandler and the dispatcher were unable to review the surveillance video because they had a prisoner in cells and it would have affected the continuity of the recording.

Cst. Chandler swears that when he opened the alleyway door, there would have been no possible way that a human being would have been able to elude him that quickly. Whether it was in fact a ghost or a person remains unknown. What is for certain is that the figure vanished without a trace.

A MURDER IN PROGRESS

In 2005, Cst. Chandler was working for another police agency within Pictou County, Nova Scotia. He recalls being in the dispatcher's office when a 911 call came into the station. Conveniently for him, he could hear the entire call which minimizes any delay in relaying information between dispatcher and officer.

The night janitor at Canada Post called to report a major disturbance in the old abandoned apartment above the post office. The janitor said it sounded like someone was being bludgeoned to death. The janitor could hear the ungodly screams of a woman and what sounded like walls being kicked in.

The post office was only 91 meters away from the police station. Cst. Chandler grabbed his female partner that was in the office and they ran out of the police station. They arrived at the post office seconds later where they were met by the janitor.

The janitor opened the door which leads to the apartment above Canada Post. The screaming had stopped at that point, but the janitor told the officers that it sounded like someone was being murdered. Cst. Chandler and his partner raced up the staircase. The janitor had a key to open the apartment door. No one was authorized to be in the apartment as it was vacant and had not been rented out for quite some time.

As the door swung open, Cst. Chandler could see that there were no lights on in the apartment. The officers drew their guns and flashlights. Cst. Chandler began screaming "POLICE!" several times, but there was no response. As Cst. Chandler and his partner did a slow and methodical search of every room in the apartment, they did not find anyone or anything. In fact, there wasn't even any furniture in the apartment.

Cst. Chandler and his partner searched every room in the apartment but there was nothing out of the ordinary. Before searching the last room, Cst. Chandler told his partner to hold on for one second. He took his flashlight and began to roll it across the floor in the room. He could see a fine layer of dust which had accumulated over time. He told her to go into the room and then come back out. She followed his instructions and upon exiting the room, he rolled his flashlight again. Cst. Chandler could clearly see his partner's boot prints in the dust.

Cst. Chandler began rolling his police flashlight across the apartment hallway and into the other rooms. The only footprints that he could see were the distinct police boots that he and his partner were wearing.

After the apartment had been properly cleared by the officers, Cst. Chandler brought the janitor into the apartment. They explained to him that there was no one in the apartment and no signs that anyone had been in the apartment. The janitor thought to himself for a second and said that the individuals must be on the roof.

There was only one way to access the roof. It was through a window in the apartment. Cst. Chandler looked at the window and told the janitor that he didn't think anyone had accessed the roof via the window, because it had been painted shut. The janitor became upset and swore that the sounds must have been coming from the roof top.

They proceeded to check the perimeter of the building, but the only ones stirring about the entire building were the two officers and the janitor. Cst. Chandler told the janitor in a respectful manner that if someone had somehow managed to jump off the roof in the amount of time that it took him and his partner to get from the police station to the post office, that chances are, no one would be able to apprehend such a person. There were no ladders or stairwells from the roof.

The janitor began shaking and all of the colour drained from his face. Cst. Chandler asked the janitor if it could have been air trapped in some of the buildings pipes. The janitor said he has been cleaning the building for 18 years and has never heard anything like that before. The janitor didn't know what it was, but he distinctly heard screaming and people pounding on the walls. There were also sounds of items being thrown.

Cst. Chandler believed him. The officers returned to the police station and began writing their reports, detailing exactly what had unfolded. The following morning, Cst. Chandler received a telephone call from the Chief of Police. He had read Cst. Chandler's report and was still chuckling to himself on the phone. Cst. Chandler told him the exact same story that was written in his police report.

The Chief began to tell him that approximately 30 years ago, a woman was murdered by a man with a bread knife in that same apartment. The Chief also informed Cst. Chandler that this was not the first time a similar report had been made about that specific apartment. The Chief said on one other occurrence, it happened during the day. The Canada Post employees were working when they began hearing crashing, banging and a female screaming from the apartment above. The police attended the apartment at that time as well, however, no one was ever found. Given the violent and untimely death of the woman, I believe that the haunting above Canada Post could be another residual haunting.

MOMMY DEAREST

Cst. Chandler's mother passed away in August 2019 after a battle with lung cancer. Approximately one week after she had passed away, he had a strange occurrence happen in his current home.

He and his two children were sound asleep in bed. His wife was away on a business trip. At approximately 5:30 a.m., he woke up to the sound of footsteps walking up the stairs. He immediately thought that it was one of his kids who had gotten out of bed. The family dog, a 90 pound German shepherd was sleeping in the bed with Cst. Chandler. The dog who doesn't particularly like strangers heard the footsteps as well. The shepherd popped his head up and began to listen intently.

As the sound of creaky floorboards continued, the shepherd began to growl as he jumped out of bed to investigate. Cst. Chandler then heard the sound of footsteps walking back down the stairs. Cst. Chandler began wondering which of his kids were out of bed. He jumped to his feet to see what was the matter. As he walked out of his bedroom, he didn't see anyone at all. The family dog was sitting at the top of the landing, wagging his tail in which he only did in the presence of a family member.

Cst. Chandler checked both of his children's bedrooms. To his surprise, they were both still asleep in their beds. As the grogginess of sleep wore off, he realized that when his children walk up and down the stairs, the floorboards don't generally creek. However, his mother who had recently passed away was slightly overweight which would cause the floorboards to creek in a similar fashion whenever she would walk up or down the staircase.

If what Cst. Chandler had experienced was in fact his mother whom had decided to come for one final visit, then this would be known as a post-mortem apparition. Post-mortem apparitions usually only occur once. They happen several hours, days, months or even years after death has occurred. The apparition usually appears to a person who is known to them such as a close friend or relative. The friend or family member usually describes a sense of peace after the experience and sometimes messages from the deceased are passed along.

Whereas he didn't specifically see his mother, or anyone else for that matter, Cst. Chandler can't say for sure that his mother came to say a final goodbye. What did intrigue him was the distinct sound of the footsteps and his loyal

shepherd acting as if he had just seen a member of the family.

His experience is indeed intriguing.

CONJURING THE DEAD

Cst. Chandler shared his origin story of how he became interested in the paranormal. It was 1996 and he was only 16 years old. He had built a cabin in the woods located in back of his primary residence. His family lived in Reserve Mines, Nova Scotia. The cabin was a very rustic shack made of logs and shift board.

One evening, he invited four of his friends to come and hang out in the cabin. One of those friends had brought an Ouija board with them. It wasn't the retail Ouija board, it was what Cst. Chandler described as being "an uncomfortable one." He said it was a homemade one that had "hell", "666" and some weird symbols burned into the plywood.

Cst. Chandler and his friends lit a candle and began playing with the Ouija board. Initially, the crew of young men were in a joking mood, however, they eventually settled down and began trying to conjure any spirits. After using the board for a while, they all began hearing footsteps outside of the cabin. It certainly changed the mood inside the cabin. The boys felt uneasy and suggested that it may be a cat or a raccoon wandering around outside. Eventually the sound of footsteps went away and nothing further happened that night.

The following day, Cst. Chandler returned to his cabin alone to clean it. As he was cleaning upstairs, the Ouija board was still there. His friend who owned it had left it there because the crew had decided to spend another night at the cabin.

Cst. Chandler looked at the board and couldn't control his curiosity. He sat down and put his fingers on the planchette. He asked the board if it was evil or good. He said it wasn't long before he felt like something had taken over his arm. The planchette began moving across the board on what seemed to be its own accord. As the planchette began sliding across the plywood Ouija board, Cst. Chandler heard a single loud pounding noise at the door of the cabin. The noise was so loud that it shook the entire cabin.

Cst. Chandler was terrified, but quickly realized that it could have been his brother in law playing a joke on him. Cst. Chandler yelled to his brother in law to come upstairs because he had gotten the Ouija board to work. He was excited at the prospect that there would be someone else to witness it working. However, after a few moments Cst. Chandler didn't hear anything else, so he peaked his head out of the upstairs window. It was a clear sunny day and his brother in law's vehicle was not parked outside.

Cst. Chandler became extremely frightened. He was so scared, that he decided he didn't want to leave his cabin through the front door. He opened the upstairs window and proceeded to climb down to the ground. As soon as his feet hit the bottom, he ran as fast as he could toward his house.

The next strange occurrence happened a week later. A couple of his friends had called him one evening and asked if he wanted to take his motorcycle out for a ride. He left his house and began walking toward his backyard where the bike was stored. It was dark outside, but that didn't bother him. He was in a good mindset and not thinking about anything related to the paranormal. Suddenly, approximately 20 feet away from him, he saw something that he hopes he never sees again… an apparition!

Standing near the barn, he saw a partial apparition. It was the lower half of a person which looked like it had been cut into two pieces by a saw. The legs were a whiteish translucent color and it was walking around the front of the barn very erratically.

Cst. Chandler was trying to process what was happening. Part of his brain was telling him that someone was trying to break into his family's barn to steal his motorcycle. The other part of his brain struggled with what he was seeing.

The partial apparition turned facing Cst. Chandler and started walking toward him. He took his motorcycle helmet and threw it as hard as he could toward the apparition. The apparition stopped approaching him, turned around and began running toward his cabin in the woods. Cst. Chandler watched the apparition run away until it faded into the abyss.

I asked Cst. Chandler if he was aware of any tragic circumstances on his property, however, he said that to his knowledge, there hadn't been any. He still thinks about this incident frequently and credits the ghost sighting to the Ouija board. He truly believes that he and his friends conjured up something negative. He believes this, because his story does not end here.

He said that after he had witnessed the severed apparition, he was continually harassed night after night by something. His bedroom was located in his parent's finished basement. When lying in bed, he could hear the distinct sound of footsteps and a slow shuffling sound approaching him. It happened no less than 12 times and the sound would stop right by the edge of his bed every single time.

He would wake up in the morning and find his bed comforter and sheets stripped off of him and bunched up on the floor. Now, Cst. Chandler is aware that people often kick their blankets off during the night when they get too warm, however in this instance, the blankets would be stuffed into a pile near his dresser which was situated approximately five feet away from his bed.

He also usually slept with his bedroom door open, but after the incident with the apparition, his bedroom door began closing on its own. The first time that it happened, he thought maybe his father had shut the bedroom door. He yelled out to his father, "Dad!, Dad!", but there was no response. He got out of bed to investigate and discovered his father sound asleep and snoring in the upstairs master bedroom.

Another time, something physically assaulted Cst. Chandler. He was walking toward his bedroom when he suddenly felt what he described as "a marble being fired out of a slingshot" or when someone flicks the back of your neck really hard. He still remembers the thud noise it made. Terrified, he ran upstairs. Thinking that it may have been his father throwing something at him, he went to inquire. His father, however, was sitting in his chair watching television with Cst. Chandler's mother. His dad had been too far away in the house to have been the culprit.

On another occasion, Cst. Chandler was awoken to a burning sensation on his arm. When he looked, he saw two long scratch marks which were hurting. He checked his bed to make sure he hadn't scratched himself on something, but he didn't find anything.

Cst. Chandler said that eventually the activity ceased on its own accord. He truly believes that the manifestations he experienced at his family home and cabin were as a result of playing with the Ouija board.

In 2020, Cst. Chandler told his story to a Roman Catholic priest in Louisburg, Nova Scotia. The priest believed that by dabbling in the occult, God had opened the gates of hell which in turn allowed a lower ranking demon to be released. After showing Cst. Chandler a glimpse of what can happen when one dabbles in the occult, God sent the demon back to hell which in turn ended the supernatural phenomena.

CALEDONIA MILLS

Nova Scotia is home to two of the most famous poltergeist cases in the world; the Great Amherst Mystery involving a female by the name of Esther Cox, and the fire-spook of Caledonia Mills involving another female by the name of Mary-Ellen MacDonald. Caledonia Mills is the lesser known of the two poltergeist cases, unless of course you are from the county of Antigonish.

Caledonia Mills is a small community within Antigonish County. The old farm house which became known as "the spook farm", was once home to Mary-Ellen MacDonald and her adopted parents, Alexander and Janet. Every year, students from St. Francis Xavier University hold a large outdoor party at the remnants of the old farm.

I have personally investigated the spook farm twice. The first time was on August 25, 2001 with the Centre for Parapsychological Studies in Canada. A small team of six investigators travelled from Halifax to Antigonish. The location is not an easy one to find. Today it is home to overgrown grass, a rock foundation, and an old well. It took us until 8:00 p.m. that evening to find the spook farm which is 13 kilometers from Croft on Highway 316. The rock foundation and old well were hidden amongst the heavy woods. After the tents were set up, three of the investigators returned to a comfortable bed and breakfast back in the small town of Saint Andrews. Investigators Angela Snair, Pierre Filiatreault and myself remained at the spook farm.

Initially, our investigative plan consisted of maintaining contact with the investigators back at the bed and breakfast. However, due to the distance between the spook farm and the bed and breakfast, neither cellular nor radio communication would work. Angela, Pierre and I were left to fend for ourselves at the spook farm. Disappointingly, none of us experienced anything unusual that night.

There is a local legend attached to the spook farm which stipulates that anyone who removes anything from the property will be cursed, and that a fire will start wherever the item is kept. Since there wasn't much left to take, I removed a piece of the foundation which has been in my possession for the past 20 years with no complications. A second investigation was discussed for the Spring of 2002, however, it never came to fruition.

(A piece of the Spook Farm foundation. Photo courtesy of Elliott Van Dusen.)

I would eventually investigate the spook farm a second time with my organization, Paranormal Phenomena Research & Investigation. I had attended the location in 2003 for reconnaissance purposes before planning a full scale investigation. The area was slightly more overgrown, but I was able to find the location. Photographs were taken at the time and we would begin planning the investigation throughout the course of the year. I'll circle back to the second investigation shortly.

The story of Mary-Ellen MacDonald and the spook farm is a classic poltergeist case, with the exception of the duration of the activity. Unlike a haunting which can last for years, poltergeist activity usually has a shorter duration, anywhere from a week and half up to a year and half. The case in Caledonia Mills lasted for 12 years beginning in 1910 and ending in 1922.

Classic parapsychological theories hypothesize that poltergeist activity is caused either by a ghost or energy emanating from a prepubescent teenager, usually a female. After decades of research, parapsychologists now believe that poltergeist activity is caused by living people, known as Mind Matter Interaction (MMI), specifically Recurrent Spontaneous Psychokinesis (RSPK). It can be manifested by one or more people living at a location, often, but not always, troubled adolescents. The events are believed to be intrinsically meaningful. Some parapsychologists believe that the poltergeist activity is a way of relieving one's stress through the physical expression of unconscious feelings.

Although poltergeist activity has similarities to a haunting, there are some unique differences. The haunting activity usually ceases if the living agent is no longer present. Spontaneous fires or water appearing, along with injuries to people are reported during poltergeist hauntings but are rare in apparitional hauntings.

Apparitions are rarely seen during a poltergeist haunting and when they are, they do not appear humanlike but are often described as dark, distorted figures. Auditory voices in poltergeist hauntings are also extremely rare. Poltergeist cases usually involve actual items being moved, thrown or breaking whereas discarnate entity investigations often report the auditory sounds of items being moved or broken. Discarnate entity hauntings tend to be more hallucinatory in nature and do not correspond to actual physical disturbances, unlike poltergeist hauntings. Now, without further ado, I present to you the facts of this case.

Mary-Ellen MacDonald was born to John and Annie MacDonald in New Glasgow, Nova Scotia. Her parents had four children. John was killed at a young age during a mining accident in Westville. Struggling to make ends meet, Annie had decided to find foster homes for her children. Annie's friends Alexander and Janet MacDonald agreed to foster two-year old Mary-Ellen in 1910.

The strange occurrences seemed to occur shortly after adopting Mary-Ellen. The MacDonald family was able to keep the strange happenings under wraps up until Mary-Ellen attended school. Interest peaked in this case occurred in 1922 at which time the MacDonald's made the decision to flee their family farm on January 7, 1922.

The first documented occurrence came from the MacDonald's neighbour Ronald MacGillivray. MacGillivray would find mats rolled up neatly and placed along the MacDonald and MacGillivray property line. The MacDonald's blamed their family dog for dragging the mats to that location, however, MacGillivray began finding cast iron pots and other household items in which he knew the dog was not physically capable of carrying.

Prior to turning in for the evening, Alexander MacDonald would tend to the barn animals and make sure they were tucked away securely. In the morning, the animals would be found untamed and roaming about freely. Alexander went to extreme lengths to curb this inconvenience by nailing the horses ropes down and even selling some of his horses in exchange for new ones. However, every morning the nails would be missing and the animals were once again set free. A skeptical Alexander didn't suspect anything too unusual was occurring until one morning when he found a horse's mane and tail had been mysteriously braided.

The nick name "fire spook" came from the 38 fires that the MacDonald's would endure in one single evening on January 7, 1922. The fires began breaking out around 5:00 p.m. and continued throughout the night until 8:00 a.m the following morning. The MacDonald's were finding rafters, furniture, ceilings, dresser drawers, wallpaper, window blinds, bedding, and even the dog's bed set ablaze. Mysterious pieces of cotton were found scattered throughout the residence which were catching on fire. The fires were also witnessed by neighbours Dan and Leo MacGillivray and Duncan MacDonald. When Duncan went into town to get additional help, Mike MacGillivray and John F. Kenny came to assist. On their way to the spook farm, they saw a small black dog trailing along behind them. When they reached the MacDonald homestead, the dog disappeared.

As Mike and John approached the farm house, they could see a bare arm with a white cloth sticking out of the upstairs window. The hand was waving the cloth back and forth as if they required assistance. As they entered the house and told the MacDonald family what they had just seen, they were surprised to learn that no one was upstairs. They proceeded to tell the MacDonald's about the black dog that they had encountered. The MacDonald's had first met this strange dog several years ago.

It was on April 27, 1900 when Janet had reached her limit of looking after her mother who was suffering from what sounded like major neurocognitive disorder. One evening, Janet yelled at her "I hope the devil in hell comes and takes you before nine o'clock tomorrow morning." She no sooner spoke the words when the same strange black dog was seen wandering inside the MacDonald household. The MacDonald's assumed it was a stray dog. It didn't bother the barn animals and Mary-Ellen would play with it on occasion. The following morning, Janet's mother had passed away.

The MacDonald's made the decision for safety reasons to vacate their property. They collected whatever belongings they could that day and moved into a house nearby which was owned by Duncan MacDonald. Alexander MacDonald would be required to attend the spook farm daily to feed the animals as they were unable to relocate them due to the heavy snow which had accumulated.

(Detective Peter Owen "Peachy" Carroll. Photo courtesy of Pictou-Antigonish Regional Library and utilized under the creative common licencing agreement.)

On January 30, 1922, Peter Owen "Peachy" Carroll developed an interest in the spook farm investigation. He was the former police chief of the Town of Pictou. He left the police force to work as a detective on the Provincial Detective Force. Det. Carroll had no experience investigating the paranormal, however, he had worked several high profile criminal cases. Det. Carroll had been following the media reports on the spook farm and believed that there was a rational explanation for the incident. He approached the spook farm investigation from a criminal investigation perspective. If this was a case of arson, Det. Carroll was determined to bring the person responsible to justice.

On February 2, 1922 Det. Carroll left Pictou for Antigonish with the intentions of staying at the MacDonald farm. Harold Whidden, who was a freelance journalist for the Halifax Chronicle Herald, agreed to stay with Det. Carroll at the spook farm.

Det. Carroll and Whidden were joined by Alexander MacDonald, Duncan MacDonald and Leo MacGillivray. Once they arrived, they set up a portable stove and prepared their sleeping arrangements. Nothing unusual occurred during their first night.

The second night Det. Carroll and Whidden were kept awake with the sounds of footsteps coming from upstairs. The two sleuths heard loud bangs which were not attributed to house settling noises. Whidden was slapped on his left arm by an unseen force and Det. Carroll felt a hand touch his left arm. Nothing else happened that evening.

The conditions at the MacDonald farm were unimaginable. There was a blizzard which had been raging onward outside. The temperature inside the house despite having the portable stove ablaze was averaging -30° Celsius. Det. Carroll, Whidden and Alexander MacDonald were starting to feel the effects of the miserable conditions. Det. Carroll and Whidden examined the MacDonald homestead from top to bottom and couldn't find any human cause for the strange noises nor the previous fires. They decided that they had endured enough of the torturous conditions at the MacDonald homestead and departed the residence.

Det. Carroll's official statement dated February 14, 1922 read:

> "After what I consider a thorough investigation, which included a careful examination of Alexander MacDonald, his wife Janet and their foster daughter

Mary-Ellen, the MacGillivray brothers, Dan and Leo, Duncan MacDonald, John F. Kenny and Mike MacGillivray, and after examining the barn very carefully, and seeing with my own eyes the scars left by the fires, some of them charred, others scorched and still others like smooches, and after spending two days and two nights in the house, I firmly believe that neither the fires nor other strange occurrences about the farm were the cause of human hands."

The MacDonald's stayed in the home of Duncan MacDonald until May of 1922. They missed their old homestead and decided to return. The first couple of weeks were uneventful. However, on May 18, 1922 fires began to break out at the MacDonald homestead again. They stayed in the house until June of 1922 at which time they made their decision to vacate the property permanently.

Alexander MacDonald would succumb to influenza on March 16, 1923. His wife Janet died on March 17, 1930. Ironically, her cause of death ... burns. As for Mary-Ellen, she was shipped around Antigonish, New Glasgow, Montreal and eventually Sudbury. Mary-Ellen passed away in 1988 at the age of 80. After the MacDonald's left the spook farm for the second time, all of the paranormal activity also ceased.

I can certainly relate to miserable conditions at the spook farm. Remember I told you that I had investigated the spook farm twice? Well on August 6, 2004 we set out with a large investigative team consisting of 10 investigators. We had initially planned on spending three evenings at the spook farm, however, the investigation became a complete disaster.

The spook farm had doubled in overgrowth from the previous year, and it took several extra hours to find the exact location. As we set up the tents in the pitch black, it began to rain heavily. Researcher Mike Shaw woke up during the middle of the night to see a huge pocket of rain water which had collected and was about to burst onto investigator Chad Murphy's head as he slept. By the time morning arrived, we were all exhausted, soaked, freezing and frustrated with one another. The series of unfortunate events led to the rest of the investigation being cancelled. Once again, nothing paranormal had occurred.

The fire spook case was also investigated by a prominent parapsychologist, Dr. Walter Franklin Prince from the American

Society for Psychical Research. Dr. Prince stayed at the old MacDonald farmstead, however, he had nothing unusual occur while he was present either. Perhaps the fire spook doesn't like parapsychologists? Dr. Prince even had Mary-Ellen attend the residence as he believed she was the living agent causing the poltergeist activity, however, nothing inexplicable happened.

Prince disagreed with Det. Carroll and believed that the fires were caused by human hands. He noted that the burns were never found on the wall paper higher than the reach of Mary-Ellen being approximately five feet in height. There were two burn marks higher up, however, Dr. Prince believed the fire had started lower and creeped up the wall toward the ceiling. Dr. Prince wrote in his report that "There were never any fires when the family, including the girl, were out of the house." Dr. Prince errored in that fact as there were actually six fires that broke out after Janet and Mary-Ellen had left to go and get help on the evening the 38 fires erupted at the spook farm. Dr. Prince found Det. Carroll and free-lance journalist Whidden to be credible and did not discount their experiences acknowledging that phenomena of this sort can be sporadic and little is known about their physical laws of nature.

The fire spook of Caledonia Mills still remains one of my favourite poltergeist cases. I suppose it is the mystery that still surrounds it to this day. Some people believe that Mary-Ellen was the cause of the commotion, not due to some preternatural cause but as an attention seeker. Others believe that Mary-Ellen was the cause but unbeknownst to her through the RSPK theory. Still, there are others who believe someone had it out for the MacDonald's and that it may have been their handy work that caused the MacDonald's to flee their home in fear. Even to this day, the rumors and folklore surrounding this case remain strong in the community of Caledonia Mills.

NEAR-DEATH EXPERIENCE

One evening in November 1982, RCMP Cpl. Karen Landry was working a patrol shift in Southern Alberta. RCMP dispatch received a report of a serious motor vehicle accident. Cpl. Landry grabbed her police radio and answered the call for service.

As she arrived on scene, she could see a vehicle resting in the ditch which had been severely damaged. A drunk driver had struck the vehicle head on which caused the collision. As she slid down the ditch and approached the vehicle, she began to realize that it was an RCMP cruiser. Taken aback, she rushed over to the vehicle and saw her friend and work partner Cst. Drew Barrington unconscious. She recognized him immediately because he was illuminated by light. After processing the fact that this was a police involved accident, Cpl. Landry sprung into action.

The steering wheel was pressed against Cst. Barrington's chest. The roof of the vehicle was caved in on top of his bleeding head. The emergency light bar on the top of the vehicle had been torn off and was found a distance away from the damaged police vehicle. The injured officer's heart rate was extremely volatile. There were times when Cpl. Landry couldn't feel his pulse. In fact, there was a medical doctor who had stopped at the scene of the accident and checked the injured officer. He grabbed Cst. Landry's arm before she approached the vehicle and told her that there was nothing further he could do for the injured officer. For all intents and purposes, the doctor on scene was unofficially declaring Cst. Barrington deceased. The paramedics who attended the scene were eventually able to resuscitate Cst. Barrington and transport him to the local hospital.

The drunk driver who had struck Cst. Barrington's vehicle was sitting on the street curb holding his head. As is the case with many impaired driving accidents, the impaired driver only had minor injuries considering his white pick-up truck had crashed head on with a police vehicle and was resting on its side.

Now that Cst. Barrington was being transported to the hospital, she completed her accident investigation. Upon returning to the RCMP Detachment, she attended the office of Traffic Services Section. Traffic Services generally assumes investigative responsibility for serious and fatal car accidents. Upon speaking to members of the unit, Cst. Landry made a shocking discovery.

The investigators had commented on the poor lighting conditions in the area. She told the investigators that there was a street light near the damaged police vehicle because she recalled Cst. Barrington being so brightly illuminated, that it was almost as though the street light was over top of him. They showed Cst. Landry their sketches and photographs and assured her that there was no street light.

She reattended the scene and discovered for herself that there were no street lights. Due to the severity of the accident, access to the road had been stopped. Thinking that it may have been headlights illuminating the body of Cst. Barrington, she repositioned her vehicle only to discover that the damaged police vehicle would have been too far down the embankment for headlights to illuminate his body. She attributed this illumination to Cst. Barrington's soul leaving his body.

The medical team caring for Cst. Barrington told the RCMP that they weren't sure if Cst. Barrington would survive. He was in grave condition. However, after spending several days in the intensive care unit, Cst. Barrington would eventually be declared stable. He would later be required to undergo intense physiotherapy.

Several weeks after the accident, Cpl. Landry received a surprise visit from Cst. Barrington and his wife. With a bottle of wine in hand, Cst. Barrington thanked Cpl. Landry for all that she had done for him. He told Cpl. Landry that he had seen her at the accident scene with him. He said that he was floating outside of his body, hovering above the accident scene, watching Cpl. Landry from a bird's eye view. Cst. Barrington knew Cpl. Landry was comforting him during the incident.

Cpl. Landry recently met with Cst. Barrington in November 2020 and asked him if he recalled his near-death experience from 38 years ago. Unfortunately, due to several head injuries over the years he was unable to recall the incident.

Cpl. Landry recalls the incident vividly as she told me it had a life changing impact on her in relation to her belief about life after death. Where the incident was extremely traumatic and involved a close personal friend and partner of hers, she suffers from post-traumatic stress disorder. I commended her on wanting to share this extraordinary experience with us.

OUIJA BOARD POSSESSION

(The Ouija board used during the séance. Photo courtesy of MCpl. Andrew Baird.)

I was intrigued to learn that my brother-in-law Master Corporal (MCpl.) Andrew Baird who was kind enough to share several other stories with us in *Supernatural Encounters: True Paranormal Accounts from Law Enforcement,* had neglected to tell me about this experience. This story came to my attention from retired MCpl. Auburn White of the Canadian military who was kind enough to share the next set of stories with us.

MCpl. White was a military police officer posted to 15 Wing Moose Jaw Air base in Saskatchewan, Canada after basic training. A few months after being stationed in Moose Jaw, MCpl. White was deployed to Afghanistan. After serving seven months overseas, she was returned home to Moose Jaw.

One evening in 2009, MCpl. White attended MCpl. Baird's residence where several other military members gathered for an evening of social festivities. These were government owned homes referred to in the military as PMQs or "Personal Married Quarters". As his guests settled in, MCpl. Baird decided to break out his Ouija board.

An Ouija board, commonly referred to as a spirit board, can be custom made or purchased from some retailers. It is a board containing alphanumeric markings and usually the words "yes", "no", "hello" and "good-bye". Participants place their fingertips on a small triangle piece called the planchette which is used to answer questions from the group.

MCpl. Baird and a couple of his military guests decided to see if there were any spirits present. As their fingers rested upon the planchette, it began spelling out the word "poo skin". They looked at one another with confusion upon their faces. Poo skin? What on Earth is poo skin? Suddenly MCpl. Baird saw his friend Travis who was sitting next to him, turn pale and almost appeared to be in shock. Travis wasn't touching the planchette. His father had recently passed away and he didn't want to dabble in the occult.

MCpl. Baird asked Travis what was the matter, however, Travis didn't respond. All of the other military members also began asking Travis what was wrong. Travis finally spoke up and said that when he was younger, he had a friend who called him "poo skin" because of the number of moles he had on his arms. Travis proceeded to tell the wide eyed party goers that his friend had died when they were kids. With Travis not partaking in the Ouija board festivities and the lack of prior knowledge of this information by the other participants, a prank and subconscious movement of the planchette were ruled out.

As the evening progressed, MCpl. Baird decided that he wanted to try a séance with his Ouija board. In parapsychology, a séance is when a gathering of individuals, usually with the assistance of a medium, come together in an attempt to establish contact with the spirit world.

MCpl. White had agreed to participate as she too was an Ouija board owner and had used it many times before. No one in the group, including MCpl. Baird had ever participated in a séance before. MCpl. White sat next to MCpl. Baird on the couch. The group attempted to make contact with any spirit who maybe listening. After a period of silence, MCpl. Baird began to speak, however, his physical appearance and demeanour had changed.

MCpl. Baird turned his head slowly and his eyes fixed intently onto MCpl. White. She noticed MCpl. Baird's eyes had changed which made her feel very unsettled. They were darker in colour. His facial expression was also different. She had known MCpl. Baird for over a year and it was an expression in which she had never seen him display before.

MCpl. Baird began to speak, claiming to be an older gentleman from the 18th century. She didn't recall what questions were asked or if they even ended the session with a "Good-bye". She does vividly remember the sheer panic which overcame her. The entire 20 minute event felt like it had taken place over several hours.

MCpl. Baird hadn't realized that the session had lasted 20 minutes. To him, it only felt like a 30 second event. He recalled closing his eyes and seeing that he was sitting at an old wooden desk. There was a candle lit and he was writing some sort of letter with a quill and some old fashioned ink. He didn't get a sense that it was a military member's spirit. MCpl. Baird said it felt like a business man writing an important letter. Once the spirit was released from MCpl. Baird, he became frightened. He swore that he would never do something like that again.

I have only had one experience worth mentioning with the Ouija board. It was a positive encounter when I was approximately 16 years old. My brother Evan, sister Erin and I were trying to find our rec room television remote. We had searched everywhere, but couldn't find it. We decided to break out the Ouija board and ask if any spirits knew where the remote control was. Evan, Erin and I sat around the Ouija board with our fingers placed on the planchette. When we asked the question "Where is the television remote at?", the Ouija board spelled out "U-T-S". We asked the question several times, but the planchette kept spelling "U-T-S". We thought maybe it meant under the sofa. Unfortunately the only thing found under the couch were dust bunnies. We reconvened and thought that maybe it meant under the stairs. My parents had a little crawl space under the split entry stairwell that we used to play in occasionally. We searched under the stairs thoroughly, but again we came up empty handed. As ridiculous as it sounds, one of us had an idea to check underneath all of the sinks in the house, but that too failed to locate the controller.

The following day, my mother was cleaning the downstairs rec room. To all of our surprise, she found the remote control "under the sink" of my youngest sister Emileigh's kitchen play set. Unbeknownst to us, she had been playing with it and must have forgotten to put it back on the coffee table.

My mom takes full credit for the positive experience that we had with the Ouija board. Shortly after I had purchased it, she covertly had it blessed. I found out years later when she eventually told me the steps she took to protect me while investigating the paranormal. Not only did she bless the Ouija board, she used to hide blessed religious medallions in my sportscoat whenever I set off on an investigation. I verified the authenticity of her claim a couple of years ago when I located one of the medallions resting in one of my inside pockets.

So, what is the science behind the infamous Ouija board? Why do people say that it is evil? Why do some individuals believe that it is simply a parlour game while others believe it opens a doorway to the afterlife?

Spirit boards date back to the 1800s when they emerged during the height of the spiritualist movement. Parapsychologists have discovered that the planchette can move in response to the participants ideomotor response. This biological function resonates in the unconscious mind, and is an automatic and involuntary fine motor behavior. The ideomotor response has also been shown to affect dowsing rods, pendulums and table-turning during séances.

However, science has not been able to rule out the spiritualist theory. This is the most popular theory surrounding the Ouija board. The belief that a discarnate entity can be channelled through the board in order to communicate messages. Parapsychologists believe that when a person dies, their consciousness and personality remain as they were when they were still alive. So, if you were a kind person or a cruel person, you shall remain in the same state of consciousness in the afterlife. This leads into an explanation on why the Ouija board comes with a great abundance of caution.

If the spiritualist theory is true, the user of the board has no idea who they are actually communicating with. It is not the Ouija board itself that is dangerous, but whom is on the other side that you are communicating with. It could genuinely be your deceased love one establishing meaningful communication, or it could very well be an entity who was and remains to be a prankster.

To build upon this theory, if you believe discarnate entities exist, what about inhuman spirits or demons? A demon's sole purpose is to establish contact with a living agent, gain their trust and ultimately, one's permission to move into the possession stage. Which also brings up another point in that possessions are not always bad.

Mediums oftentimes allow themselves to become possessed by discarnate entities in order to pass along messages. You just read a true paranormal account from two military personnel who testify that one of them became temporarily possessed much like a medium does. It is for these reasons that the Ouija board has been deemed an extremely dangerous occult tool.

Suggestibility and telekinesis are also possible explanations. When a question is asked, our mind thinks of the potential response. It is therefore plausible that we are consciously or unconsciously answering the questions ourselves.

Lastly, there is certainly a religious connotation which has cast negativity upon the Ouija board and other forms of the occult. For instance, Leviticus 19:31 states "Do not turn to mediums or necromancers; do not seek them out, and so make yourselves unclean by them: I am the Lord your God." The Bible also reiterates my point about the dangers of knowing whom you are in communication with.

John 4:1 states "Beloved, do not believe every spirit, but test the spirits to see whether they are from God, for many false prophets have gone into the world."

One thing is for certain. If you are planning on communicating with the deceased, take the proper precautions and tread carefully.

WAINWRIGHT, ALBERTA UFO SIGHTING

In 2011, military police officer Auburn White had recently received her promotion to Master Corporal and was posted to Area Support Unit (ASU) in London, Ontario. The night skies in this part of Canada are etched into MCpl. White's memory. The illumination of stars twinkling above in the night sky were unprohibited from light pollution.

As a military police officer, she recalled many unidentified flying object (UFO) sightings being reported at different postings. There has been a recent movement within the field of UFOlogy to rename UFOs to UAP or unidentified aerial phenomena. Canadians report around 1,000 UFO sightings each year. The majority of UFO sightings are simply just that, an unidentified object in the sky. According to my esteemed Canadian colleague and UFOlogist Christopher Rutowski, the average UFO sighting in Canada lasts approximately 15 minutes. Sightings are usually witnessed by two individuals. Ironically many of which are police officers, pilots and other people trained in observational skills.

One of MCpl. White's first tasks after being promoted was to attend the detachment in Wainwright, Alberta to supervise a patrol shift during an army training exercise. One of the patrol members at her detachment in Wainwright had offered to drive her to Edmonton International Airport after the army exercise concluded. With that, she packed up her belongings and the departed ASU.

While driving along Highway 14, she recalled the night sky being dark and full of stars. There was music playing in the patrol car and as she glanced out the passenger side window, she noticed a single round red light hovering stationary in the night sky. It was small but would occasionally move at a high rate of speed in different directions. She wasn't going to say anything to the military police officer driving her, but he too eventually noticed the object. They both tried to figure out what it could be. In fact, they discussed the object for over two hours while on route to Edmonton. They both knew it wasn't an airplane, helicopter, drone or laser pointer. The object only lasted about 30 seconds before disappearing rapidly into the night sky. To this day, MCpl. White said she still regrets not taking a video of the UFO with her mobile phone.

BLUE EYES

MCpl. Auburn White at the Meaford Tank Range
(Photo courtesy of MCpl. White.)

This next story takes place on the Meaford Tank Range located in Ontario, Canada. The training area is riddled with old stone ruins and abandoned foundations of farms long since passed. It makes it a perfect training location for the Canadian Army Reserves.

MCpl. Auburn White attended this location for advanced weapons and tactical training during the solider qualification course. She had completed basic training but had not yet received her military police training.

In October 2006, she was in the field with her platoon and sergeant conducting night watch. The platoon was trained to set up trip wires and explosives. As the night wore on, the temperature dropped below zero degrees Celsius. MCpl. White's sergeant warned the platoon that their night time training was extremely rigorous, and has been known to break the morale of soldiers. Between the hunger and sleep deprivation, many soldiers beforehand have described seeing a little girl walk through the field, sometimes with a set of blue glowing eyes. The sergeant assured the soldiers that she was safe to talk too, should one of them stumble across her.

Most of the platoon members looked at each other and then chuckled. As the evening wore on, many of the soldiers did begin to hallucinate, but "Blue Eyes" as the ghost is often referred to, never made an appearance. Other Canadian Forces personnel have reported seeing apparitional figures appear and disappear while wearing night vision goggles. Others have reported hearing the desperate cries of a little girl calling for help.

Canadian Forces personnel are not allowed to enter grave sites located in the training area out of respect for the dead. However, there is a gravestone located at the Meaford Tank Range belonging to May Williams who died on June 26, 1890 at the age of seven.

Local legend states that May was outside picking flowers as

she was waiting for her mother to finish cooking dinner. When dinner was ready, her mother called out to her. As May began running home, she stepped on an old boarded up water well which collapsed causing her to fall into it. She was able to stay afloat for several hours before eventually succumbing to hypothermia. While struggling for her life, her screams for help went unanswered. Is May the glowing blue eyed apparition that Canadian Forces personnel see roaming the training fields of Meaford calling for help?

Unfortunately, little is known outside of local lore about how May Williams actually died. Her gravestone is protected by a chain link fence at the Meaford Tank Range which reads "She has gone to heaven before us, But she turns and waves her hand, Pointing to the glories o'er us, in the fair and happy land." Whether May is the mysterious "Blue Eyes" apparition or not, one fact is for certain. A child's passing is always too soon. May whosever soul wanders the Meaford Tank Range find peace.

STRANGE ENCOUNTER ON WOOD LILLY DRIVE

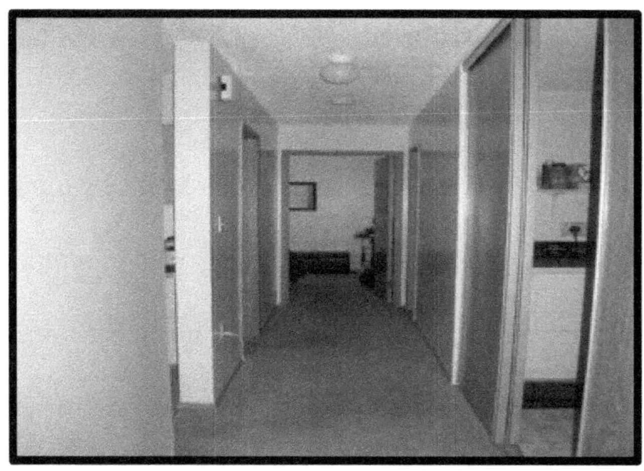

(The black leather chest where the Ouija Board materialized can be seen at the end of the hallway. Photo courtesy of M/Cpl. White.)

While posted to 15 Wing Moose Jaw Canadian Forces base, MCpl. Auburn White was required to work shift work as a military police patrol member. The posting was very taxing for a shift worker. Imagine trying to sleep during the day with the constant sound of engine start-ups from the Snowbird CT-114 Tutors, CT-156 Harvard II's, and CT-155 Hawks. MCpl. White said that when the CF-18 Hornets came to the base, all of her picture frames would fall off of her wall. She eventually made the decision to move out of government housing and found a two bedroom apartment on Wood Lilly Drive.

The apartment was older but it offered MCpl. White the

privacy and quietness she was seeking. During her off time, she would often invite friends over for game nights. MCpl. White developed a love for board games. The Ouija board was always a hit at her parties.

In the winter of 2010, MCpl. White received a transfer to her home town in London, Ontario. She was ecstatic to be returning home. She travelled to London, Ontario to make arrangements for new living accommodations. When she returned, the air base scheduled the moving company.

During the last night of MCpl. White's stay at her apartment, she went to bed a little earlier in anticipation of the early morning arrival of the moving company. During the middle of the night, she was awoken to an extremely loud noise.

Where it was the middle of the night, MCpl. White became concerned that someone was attempting to break into her apartment. She turned on her bedroom light and looked around, but she did not notice anything out of the ordinary. Her heart began to race as she made her way through the apartment. She turned on the hallway light, proceeded by the kitchen light but still did not see anything. She continued through the apartment turning on the front door entrance light, living room light and laundry room light. Everything appeared to be in order. The last room to check was the spare room.

She opened the spare bedroom door and flicked on the light. Her heart began to pound in her chest when she looked straight ahead and saw her leather chest box was wide open and the Ouija board sitting on top of it. She left the room, grabbed her purse and shoes and left the apartment in the dead of night.

She sat in her vehicle until she could compose herself. The Ouija board was always stored inside the leather chest at the very bottom, underneath all of her other board games. She specifically did this because it was the largest box out of all of her other board games. She also preferred it to be at the bottom of her storage chest due to her subconscious fear of the board game. To this day, she has no idea what the loud noise was, or how the board game ended up on top of the other games with the chest door wide open.

One theme that became evident while writing this book was certain individuals having multiple paranormal experiences. Why are some individuals more susceptible to paranormal occurrences than others? Some individuals are more perceptive and sensitive to their environments than others. Believers have statistically been shown to have more experiences than skeptics. Thanks to the work of the late

Dr. Michael Persinger, we know that paranormal beliefs and experiences are related. There is a strong correlation between the proportions of paranormal experiences that one reports and their beliefs in the paranormal. Another independent study conducted by Dr. Neil Dagnall confirmed Dr. Persinger's findings that belief in the paranormal is positively correlated with having multiple supernatural experiences. Dr. Dagnall was able to determine that gender does not make a difference when it comes to experiencing multiple subjective paranormal occurrences.

OUT OF BODY EXPERIENCE

(The bedroom where the out of body experience occurred. Photo courtesy of M/Cpl. White.)

In 2010, M/Cpl. Auburn White was posted to London, Ontario as a patrol member with the Military Police. She was very pleased when she found a reasonably priced, two bedroom apartment to rent. It came with a nice bonus as it was located directly above the Tasty Cup Coffee. The building was old, had cold drafts and was located along a busy and noisy street, but it had been recently renovated and M/Cpl. White adjusted quickly.

On one particular evening, something strange happened to M/Cpl. White. As she was sleeping, she had an out of body experience (OBE). She became consciously aware that she was floating above her sleeping body. As she looked around her bedroom, she could see herself sleeping on her back and tucked under her blankets.

After a few moments, she became very unsettled and wanted to wake up, but she was unable to. The experience became even stranger when she suddenly saw a heavy-set man sitting at the end of her bed. She was able to lower herself down and sit next to him on the bed. The heavy-set man did not speak which made M/Cpl. White feel very uneasy. She once again tried to force herself to wake up.

She eventually managed to return to her body. As she awoke, she found herself unable to physically move. She was frozen in her bed and felt a heavy weight on her chest. She kept telling herself to wake up. She felt the presence of a dark shadow in the right corner of her bedroom near the door, but she was not able to move. She tried to see over her right shoulder, but it was physically impossible. As she lay wide awake and panicking, she felt something press on her chest which hurt. She needed help immediately but could only lay there helplessly. She was so scared that she could feel tears streaming down her face. She tried to open her mouth to scream, but nothing was happening.

After several agonizing minutes, she was able to move her body. She reached for her phone and called her step mother. She was crying uncontrollably and couldn't understand what had just happened. She feared sleeping after that incident and now has to sleep on her side instead of her back.

M/Cpl. White has undergone two sleep studies in Toronto, Ontario and she has never been diagnosed with any sleep-wake medical conditions which would account for her experience. In fact, M/Cpl. White wasn't even aware of astral projection or sleep paralysis until a few years after her OBE experience. Astral projection is simply another term used to describe out of body travel. Based on M/Cpl. White's lived experience, it certainly seems indicative of a genuine out of body experience.

In parapsychology, OBEs are when an individual's consciousness leaves the physical body. This is similar to a near-death experience (NDE) only in that the human consciousness has reportedly left the physical body. OBEs can be both controlled or spontaneous, whereas NDEs mostly occur during the final stage of the death process before it becomes irreversible, known as clinical death or the cessation of a person's vital functions. OBE experiencers often times report being in the vicinity of their physical body while observing their immediate environment from above. Although rare, some OBE experiencers have reported seeing a discarnate entity during their OBE such as the heavy-set man witnessed by M/Cpl. White. The paralysis she described is also a common sensation often reported during the termination portion of the OBE. This is known as catalepsy which is a lack of bodily sensation or control often accompanied with complete rigidity.

Sleep paralysis has also been reported in other paranormal phenomena such as incubus and succubus visits, alien abductions and demonic possession. Generally, sleep paralysis is a medical condition in which elements of wakefulness and rapid eye movement (REM) sleep become intertwined. This results in a rather terrifying state in which one is not able to voluntarily move all the while being perceptually awake. Sleep paralysis can be accompanied by visual hallucinations which can evoke a strong feeling of fear. Some percipients have reported the feeling of an intruder or sensing an evil presence, the feeling of pressure on the chest, suffocation or physical pain. Not all OBEs are negative however. Some individuals claim to be able to enter an OBE state on command and at their own free will.

SLEEPLESS IN VICTORIA

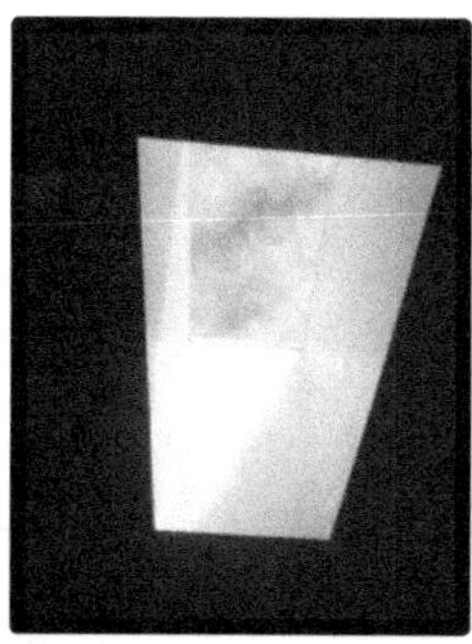

(Left: 3610 Richmond Road, Victoria, British Columbia. Right: The skylight in the ensuite bathroom. Photos courtesy of M/Cpl. White.)

During the summer of 2011, M/Cpl. White had been transferred to the Canadian Forces Base in Esquimalt, British Columbia as a Military Police patrol supervisor. She managed to secure a corner unit at a newer apartment building situated at 3610 Richmond Road in Victoria. The rent was expensive, but it had an incredible view of Mount Tolmie. It wouldn't be long after she moved into her new apartment, that she would experience some strange happenings.

Her bedroom ensuite bathroom was a beautiful bright space with a big skylight on the ceiling. It came with some unexpected visitors however. She could hear strange tapping coming from the bathroom. When she looked above her, she saw several black crows standing on her skylight staring down. The crows were relentless, tapping on the glass skylight watching her every day over the span of a year.

The shiftwork that M/Cpl. White endured began taking a toll on her sleep. She worked many nightshifts which would then require her to sleep during the daytime. On one particular day, she fell asleep rather quickly. She suddenly had the feeling that she needed to wake up. As she attempted to wake herself up, she opened her eyes only to find that she couldn't move her head or body at all. She could see her bedroom and recalls the sunlight beaming in through the window. She had the same feeling of fear as she did the time before in London, Ontario during her OBE. She didn't feel any pressure on her chest this time, but all she could do was lay in bed helplessly. She reported a strong feeling of a presence in the room, which as we discussed previously, is a common characteristic of sleep paralysis.

As she lay in bed, tears began to stream down her face. Similar to before she wasn't able to open her mouth or speak. She was literally stuck in bed with nothing but her own thoughts. After a few more minutes, she was finally able to move. Having had this happen to her twice, M/Cpl. White was at a crossroads in her life. She developed great anxiety about falling asleep for fear that another sleep paralysis episode would occur. She was eventually released from the military and returned home to London, Ontario. She is happy to report that she has not encountered any other episodes of sleep paralysis since her time in Victoria.

BURNING BRIGHT

(The two candles that Harold Feiertag had lit in memory of his wife Clare twenty four hours after her death. The heavy star weight which was thrown across the room can be seen in the middle. Photo courtesy of Harold Feiertag.)

Wanting to share his experiences, retired Cst. Harold Feiertag contacted my colleague Dr. Darryll Walsh at Ghost Project Canada. Being a retired RCMP officer myself, Dr. Walsh felt it was only appropriate that I speak with Cst. Feiertag. As it turned out, Cst. Feiertag and I both attended the RCMP training academy from January through to July, albeit 31 years in the difference. He had commenced his training in 1974, while I attended in 2005.

On March 28, 2013 at 11:35 p.m., Cst. Feiertag's wife Clare passed away from Non-Hodgkin lymphoma cancer. She lived for 25 weeks after receiving her diagnosis. The death of any person we love is a tragic event that we all must endure at some point in time. However, Clare was Cst. Feiertag's soulmate and her death shook him to the absolute core of his being.

The following morning after Clare's death, his daughter Jannette came to his house on Santa Monica Drive in North Delta, British Columbia to stay with him for a while. She wanted to offer her love, support and help make any needed arrangements. Clare was Janette's step-mother. His other daughter Brittney lived with him and was the biological daughter of Clare. Cst. Feiertag was very happy to have his two daughters by his side during this difficult time. He told Janette that later in the evening, 24 hours after Clare had passed to be exact, he was going to light a candle in her honour.

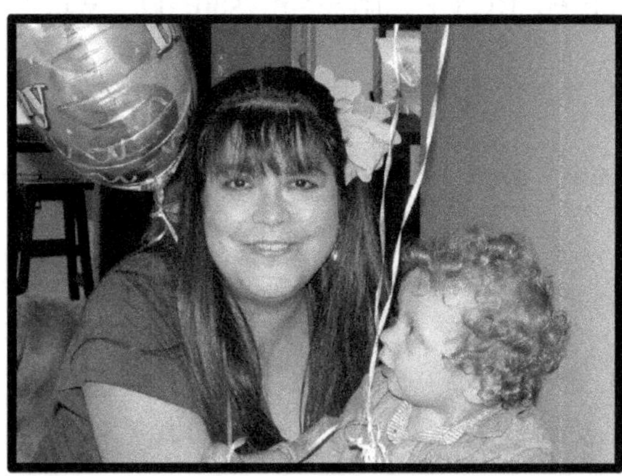

(Clare Feiertag with her step grandson Daxon. Photo courtesy of Harold Feiertag.)

On his buffet, he had two candles each housed in a crystal

candle holder. At 11:35 p.m., he lit the left candle in memory of Clare. He decided that he might as well light the candle on the right. After both of the candles were lit, Cst. Feiertag could feel a tear stream down his face. He noticed that the candle on the left was shining just a little bit brighter than the candle on the right. He said "Clare, you are the candle on the left because you have always outshined everyone on Earth."

He entered the kitchen and plugged in his kettle to make some instant coffee. As he returned to the buffet with the candles, his eyes became as wide as saucers. The candle on the left had remained the same, but the candle on the right now had a flame shooting out of it. The flame was between 11 and 12 inches in height. He rushed around his house to find a candle snuffer. After locating it, he snuffed out both candles and began wondering what that was all about. He would later come to believe that Clare was trying to show him that he is brighter than what he thinks.

Rattled, he went to his back door and lit a cigarette. As he was standing in front of his kitchen cupboards, something flew off of the shelf, hit the counter, and landed on the floor. He bent over and picked the item up. It was a weighted star that was used to keep helium balloons from flying away. He examined the shelf where the star was kept and was unable to determine how the object was thrown from where it had been stored.

He put the star back where it belonged and decided to turn in for the evening. He fell asleep on the couch downstairs and had one of the most restful sleeps in months. At 7:30 a.m., his daughter Janette came out of the bedroom and sat on the love seat. His other daughter Brittney sat next to him. He proceeded to tell his daughters about the out of control candle flame and the flying star from the night before.

When he said the star flew off the shelf and hit the floor, his daughter Brittney began to cry uncontrollably. Cst. Feiertag understood that she had just lost her mother, but he wasn't expecting that strong of an emotional reaction form Brittney. He put his arms around her. Janette came over and also embraced her. Cst. Feiertag asked her what was wrong.

"Dad, last night, I asked mom to give me a sign that she was in heaven with the stars," she said as she stared up at the ceiling with tears streaming down her face.

Wow," responded Cst. Feiertag.

He told Brittney that she had gotten her sign. Cst. Feiertag unequivocally believes that Clare was present in spirit that particular evening.

Cst. Feiertag has had other strange occurrences happen to him involving Clare. Cst. Feiertag is a wild-life photographer and while Clare was sick in the hospital, she would encourage him to get outside and photograph nature. She was very encouraging of him to photograph the snowy owl. Cst. Feiertag did manage to take some photographs of a snowy owl. Before Clare passed away, Cst. Feiertag submitted one of the pictures of the snowy owl to meteorologist Kristie Gordon on Global News. As the weeks went by, he never heard anything further about his photograph.

On April 5, 2013 Clare was cremated. When Cst. Feiertag returned home with his two daughters, one of his friends called him. The friend was ecstatic and said he had been watching the news and Kristie Gordon had just showed his snowy owl picture. He didn't believe it at first, because so much time had gone by since he had first submitted it. Clare was always supportive of Cst. Feiertag and he believes that this was a message from Clare to continue his pursuit and love of photography.

On Valentine's Day in 2014, the first Valentine's Day since

Clare's passing, Cst. Feiertag was finding it to be a particularly difficult day. Later in the morning, he turned on the radio and the song "*Unchained Melody*" by *The Righteous Brothers* began playing. The year before, on Valentine's Day, Clare had given Cst. Feiertag a Valentine's Day card and when it was opened, the song "*Unchained Melody*" would play.

Swiss psychiatrist and psychoanalyst Carl Jung believed in synchronicity. In nature there exists a tendency for two separate systems to conform to a common structure or to coincide. Jung believed it was not a casual process but an acasual one where one system was not being physically linked to the other system or mechanistically causing the latter to conform with it in some degree. He hypothesized that certain experiences are instances of synchronicity or meaningful coincidences.

Cst. Feiertag had offered the star to his daughter Brittney, but she felt it was more appropriate for him to hang onto it. To this day, he keeps the weighted star and candle holders near to his heart.

THE SCREAMING PRISONER

(Cape Breton Correctional Facility. Photo by Elliott Van Dusen.)

Ariah Harlen is a supervisor for Corrections Service Canada at the Cape Breton Correctional Facility. This medium security institution has been in operation since 1975 and has the capacity to house up to 96 adult males. The institution also provides temporary accommodations to a small number of adult women and youth pending their transfers to court, the women's institution or the youth institution respectively.

Being a supervisor of a correctional facility involves a lot of administrative paperwork. That is why when supervisor Harlen was approached by a couple of his correctional officers who wanted to report a strange incident to him, his ears immediately perked up. Pushing aside the stack of paperwork on his desk, he was attentively waiting to be debriefed by the officers.

They began telling supervisor Harlen that last night, one of the female prisoners kept screaming that there was someone else in her cell. When the correctional officers attended to her complaint, there was no one else in her cell and everything appeared to be in order. This event didn't seem to faze supervisor Harlen. It is quite possible she was experiencing some mental health distress. There have been many studies conducted which have established a correlation between mental health disorders and criminal offenders.

The correctional officers said that the female prisoner continued to alert corrections staff throughout the evening that there was someone else in her cell and that this person would not stop starring at her. She begged the correctional officers to either remove the other prisoner or change her cell. Having checked her cell multiple times and confirming that there was no one else in there, the correctional officers also assumed that she was having a mental health crisis.

As the evening wore on, meal trays were being delivered to the prisoners. The female prisoner was huddled into the corner of her cell. She left her meal tray untouched and lying on the floor. A few moments later, the female prisoner was screaming for help again. The correctional officers attended her cell to see what was wrong this time. The female prisoner said that the other prisoner had caused her food tray to slide across the floor towards her.

Supervisor Harlen asked the correctional officers if they had checked the security cameras.

"We did," said the unnerved correctional officer.

"Well?" said supervisor Harlen in anticipation.

"You had better come see for yourself Sir," he said.

Supervisor Harlen and the two correctional officers made their way to the monitoring room. One of the correctional officers queued the video recording. As they clicked on the play button, supervisor Harlen watched the screen intently. The video clearly showed that there was only a single female prisoner present in the cell. As supervisor Harlen kept watching the screen, he suddenly saw the meal tray slide violently across the cell block floor toward the female prisoner.

Supervisor Harlen was intrigued but asked if the correctional officers had checked whether or not the air exchange system had been on at the time. They acknowledged that they hadn't conducted a thorough follow up. Supervisor Harlen began checking to see which doors were accessed in the area and at which time. He also checked to see if the air exchange system had been in operation. To his disbelief, no one had opened any doors at the time the tray slid across the floor which ruled out a cross breeze. The air exchange system was also not in operation. Supervisor Harlen went as far as physically inspecting the cell and cell door, but he found nothing unusual.

Supervisor Harlen made it clear to me that he is skeptical when it comes to the supernatural, but that neither he nor the two correctional officers could explain what was captured on video surveillance. One thing that is for certain… the female prisoner was more than happy to be transferred from her cell when morning arrived.

SPONTANEOUS HUMAN COMBUSTION

Our next supernatural case comes from the archives of the Federal Bureau of Investigation (FBI). We are stepping back in time on this case to July 2, 1951 in St. Petersburg, Florida.

At approximately 8:00 a.m., Mrs. Pansy Carpenter was approached by a Western Union delivery man inquiring about what apartment number Mrs. Mary Hardy Reeser resided in. As the landlady, she offered to take the telegram to Mrs. Reeser's apartment situated at unit 1 - 1200 Cherry Street North East. Upon arrival to her unit, Mrs. Carpenter found Mrs. Reeser's apartment door partially open. As Mrs. Carpenter touched the doorknob to Mrs. Reeser's apartment, she could feel an unusual amount of heat emanating from it. Her intuition told her to telephone the police. She was not wrong.

The St. Petersburg Police Department received Pansy Carpenter's call at 8:07 a.m. The police arrived on scene shortly afterward to find what appeared to be a deceased body in a living room chair. The chair had been completely burned away, leaving only the metal springs. An end table next to the chair had also been completely burned except for two of its legs. The attending officers were standing in the living room starring at a pile of ashes. The only visible human remains that could be seen was a partial left foot with a shoe attached to it, a spine, and a skull. The walls and ceilings showed signs of extreme heat and were covered in soot. The plastic wall light switches had melted onto the floor. An electric clock had stopped at 4:20 a.m. The body would later be confirmed to be that of 67 year-old Mrs. Reeser.

The St. Petersburg Police Department chief Jacob Riley "Jake" Reichert contacted the FBI for assistance. A box of evidence was sent to Washington, D.C. to be analyzed by the FBI forensic laboratory. The evidence included: glass fragments found in the ashes, six small objects believed to be teeth, metal from near the body, fibers believed to be part of a nightgown, particles of bones found in the ashes, charred fabric from the chair, cotton material from the chair, charred wood, charged legs from the end table, charred fabric from the rug, unburned section of the rug soaked in some sort of grease, remainder of ashes, a shoe still intact from the left foot, and springs from the chair.

The initial theory the police had involved Mrs. Reeser falling asleep in her cotton-stuffed chair and accidentally setting fire to it, however, because of the intense heat which almost consumed her entire body," that theory, along with a suicide, were eliminated. Morticians advised the police that it would take hours of 1500°F to 2000°F heat to cremate a body. In Chief Reichert's memorandum dated July 7, 1952 to the FBI, he wrote "We request any information or theories that could explain how a human body could be so destroyed and the fire confined to such a small area and so little damage done to the structure of the building and the furniture in the room not even scorched or damaged by smoke."

The FBI forensic laboratory found "no oxidizing chemicals, petroleum hydrocarbons, or other volatile fluids commonly used as accelerants, or any chemical substances used to initiate or accelerate combustion." The forensic specialists did note that this doesn't mean one of those items were not used. They specified that as a result of the severe combustion in this particular case, those fluids would likely not be found. The grease that soaked the unburnt rug was discovered to be human fat.

FBI forensic specialists said that there have been a number of cases on record, which at first glance, appear to be from spontaneous combustion or preternatural causes. In all of the cases, the human body was almost completely destroyed as a result of fire. In all of the cases that they examined, no evidence was ever discovered that suggested anything other than the fire being caused by some external means such as burning clothes, bedding, or furniture. The fat and other inflammable substances in the body act as fuel for the fire which can result in almost complete combustion. This is known as the wick effect, where the body acts much like a wick from a candle.

In Mrs. Reeser's case, the FBI forensic laboratory believed that the fire had smouldered rather than burning freely which resulted in the heat liberated by the burning body to rise and form a layer of hot air which never came in contact with the furnishings. The fire reached a temperature of no less than 1000°F. The small objects believed to be teeth were identified as five teeth and one part of a denture. The metal located near her body was suspected to be metal from either a lighter or a hearing aid.

Throughout the course of the investigation, the St. Petersburg Police detectives had learned that Mrs. Reeser was prescribed Seconal, a barbiturate drug sometimes used as a sleeping pill. Her son provided a statement to the police saying that his mother had taken two Seconal before he left her apartment that evening and she told him that she had planned on taking two more before bed. The official FBI theory surrounding the death of Mrs. Reeser was that she had fallen unconscious while smoking. As a result, the cigarette set fire to her nightgown and her body fat acted as a fuel source resulting in her combustion.

Do you think the FBI's theory is plausible, or do you think Mrs. Reeser succumbed to spontaneous human combustion? Chief Reichert has been quoted as saying "This is the most unusual case I've seen during my almost 25 years of police work in the City of St. Petersburgh." What are your thoughts on this case, partner?

THE SCARRED POLICEMAN

(A sketch of the scarred policeman. Photo courtesy of Wayne Lowden.)

In the South East part of England is the historic royal county of Berkshire. This ancient community is rife with ghost stories, mythological creatures, hidden treasure, witchcraft, and folklore. All of the stories in which I have presented to you from this book and *Supernatural Encounters: True Paranormal Accounts from Law Enforcement* have been accounts from individuals in the law enforcement, security and military community. This is a unique story that I stumbled across when conducting research for this book. It involves the ghost of a police officer!

It has been reported that a Berkshire policeman with a badly scarred face still walks his former beat along the junction of the A30, A329 and the A332 in the small town of Ascot. He is usually only seen at night when the headlights of passersby illuminate his spectral figure. The unknown police officer has been described as wearing a 20th century high-necked policing tunic. Witnesses who have seen this phantom think that he may have been involved in a horrible accident, based on his disfigured face.

Other witnesses have reported seeing the scarred police officer with only half of a face in Bracknell near the railway arch between Martins Lane and Whistley Close.

The royal county of Berkshire is now policed by the Thames Valley Police department. I applied under the Freedom of Information Act and requested any information they hold pertaining to this mysterious disfigured police officer. Unfortunately, they replied that their records are not held in an easily retrievable format. They would have to manually review every incident record both past and present in electronic and hard copy format which would not be feasible for them to do so. The identity of the scarred policeman and the circumstances surrounding his death remain unknown.

LOWER SACKVILLE UFO SIGHTING

On October 16, 1976 at 11:45 p.m., Mrs. Percy Webster telephoned the Lower Sackville Royal Canadian Mounted Police detachment requesting police attendance. When the dispatcher asked for further details, Mrs. Webster advised that there was an unidentified flying object over her house situated at 39 Hillside Drive.

The RCMP dispatched Constable Pharand to investigate. When Cst. Pharand arrived, he knocked on the front door of the Webster residence. When Mrs. Webster answered, Cst. Pharand asked her to step outside to look at not one UFO, but three UFOs hovering approximately 500 feet overhead.

Mrs. Webster advised that she and her husband had been watching the UFO for quite some time. She said that earlier the UFO had appeared to be round and cigar shaped with four lights and a flat bottom with three long windows. The Websters' said at one point during their observation, they saw the objects appear to stack on top of one another for approximately two minutes before they split apart again.

Cst. Pharand and Mrs. Webster watched the objects for an extended period of time. While Cst. Pharand sat in his patrol car trying to get in touch with the Halifax International Airport, Mrs. Webster went inside to make coffee. Halifax International Airport did not have any aircraft showing up on radar over Lower Sackville. Cst. Pharand decided to check with the Canadian Forces base in Shearwater. However, the military advised that they too did not have any aircraft showing up on radar over Lower Sackville.

Cst. Pharand radioed the other RCMP officers working in the area. He asked if they could see the objects in the sky and they were able to confirm the sighting. With the assistance of the Webster's binoculars, Cst. Pharand noticed that the objects were round in shape and had red flashing lights on the bottom along with a flashing white light. There was also a stable green coloured light which appeared to be located inside the objects. Initially, the objects were stationary, however, they eventually began to move and when they did, the lights changed to a turquoise color. As the UFOs began to move, their altitude became greater. There was no sound or smell in the environment at the time and the night sky was clear.

The Webster's neighbours, Mr. and Mrs. Robert Bedford also witnessed the UFO sighting. After watching the objects for approximately two hours, Cst. Pharand had to attend another call for service. He wrote in his official police report the following:

> "I might add it is the opinion of the writer that there is no possibility at all that what I saw might have been stars or even another planet as I was looking through the binoculars and therefore, would have been able to tell the difference."

Several years later, in 1994 my colleague, UFO investigator and researcher Chris Styles, attended the residence of Mrs. Webster. Her husband had passed away, but she recalled the evening in question and was more than willing to discuss her sighting with Mr. Styles. She said she has been searching the night sky ever since 1976 hoping to see another UFO, but she never did. She was absolutely certain that the objects she saw on the evening of October 16, 1976 was in no way conventional aircraft.

Mr. Styles asked about her neighbors the Bedfords'. Mrs. Webster's demeanour quickly shifted. She advised that the Bedfords' were not home and that it wouldn't be helpful to speak to them. This naturally peaked Mr. Styles interest as a dedicated and thorough

UFOlogist. Mrs. Webster advised that they were serious Christians and she and her husband never got along very well with the Bedfords'.

Mr. Styles went next door to speak with Mr. and Mrs. Bedford, however, there was nobody home. He would spend the next couple of weeks trying to call them with the phone number listed in the official RCMP report. Finally, after several weeks of trying the phone number, a male voice answered. Mr. Styles identified himself and asked to speak to Robert Bedford. The male voice on the other end of the phone advised that he was Robert Bedford. Mr. Styles explained to him that he would like to discuss his UFO sighting from 1976. Mr. Bedford said that he didn't know what he was talking about and stated that he had never seen anything like that before.

Mr. Styles began thinking about the warning he had received from Mrs. Webster. Mr. Bedford asked where Mr. Styles had received his information. Mr. Styles explained that he had a copy of the RCMP report and had spoken to Mrs. Webster. As soon as Mr. Bedford heard the name, he immediately became dismissive advising that the Websters' could see anything.

Putting aside the testimony from the Websters', Mr. Styles reminded Mr. Bedford that several RCMP officers had also witnessed the UFO sighting that evening. Mr. Bedford responded by saying that he wasn't sure if he and his wife were living on Hillside Drive in 1976.

All of a sudden, Mr. Styles could hear Mrs. Bedford asking her husband who was on the telephone. Mr. Bedford said that it was a gentleman asking about the UFO sighting the Websters' had allegedly witnessed. To Mr. Styles surprise, he could hear Mrs. Bedford say "That was the night! You remember dear, that was the night." Mr. Styles could hear the receiver of the phone become muffled as if someone was covering the speaker.

Mr. Bedford apologized and said that he was starting to recall the incident. Excited, Mr. Styles asked him if he did see the UFO. Mr. Bedford sheepishly admitted that he had not seen the UFO because he and his wife were too afraid and had hid under their bed for the duration of the sighting.

Mr. Bedford's experience with the UFO was much different than that of the Websters' and the RCMP officers. Mr. Bedford stated that when the sighting had begun, there was an extremely loud roaring noise that shook their entire house. Mr. Bedford explained that he was a naval architect who was very familiar with conventional aircraft but he had never heard an aircraft make noise like that before.

Mr. Styles asked how he came to interact with the police officer that evening. Mr. Bedford said that as quickly as the roaring noise began, it was as if someone flicked a light switch and it immediately ceased. Mr. Bedford heard a knock at his door, so he went downstairs to find Cst. Pharand standing on his door step. Cst. Pharand asked Mr. Bedford to come outside to look at the UFO, but he politely declined. When Mr. Styles asked him what he thought the UFO could be, he responded "I don't know. I don't want to know."

Chris Styles is an extremely experienced UFO investigator. He believes this to be one of the most genuine UFO sightings that he has ever investigated. It is a lesser known case because the witnesses didn't share their experience with any media outlets. In fact, the only way this case came to light was by Mr. Styles finding the police report and personally following up with the witnesses.

Both the Bedfords' and the Websters' are considered reliable witnesses, yet reported significantly different experiences. Mr. Styles believes both of their accounts to be true and accurate. This can happen to police officers as well during their criminal investigations. Witness contamination, conscious and unconscious biases, and memory recall are just a few things that can influence one's perception. Nonetheless, this UFO sighting remains unexplained.

THE JUVENILE

(Columbia Juvenile Detention Center. Photo courtesy of Dedrick Hilton.)

Dedrick Hilton was one of the most interesting members of the law enforcement community that I have ever interviewed. He and I both studied courses at the Rhine Education Center, were Corporal's before retiring from law enforcement, and are paranormal investigators. Cpl. Hilton is currently working on his Ph.D. in metaphysical science and is a Hoodoo specialist. Hoodoo is the spiritual practice of magic, traditions and beliefs prevalent in the Southern United States of America. It was created by enslaved Africans.

Cpl. Hilton was a nighttime supervisor at the Columbia Juvenile Detention Center in South Carolina. He was responsible for physically and administratively processing all of the new juvenile inmates. When he wasn't processing inmates, he was responsible for the safety of the prisoners by conducting rounds in the cell block. He was also responsible for supervising the other correctional officers on shift. While working at the correctional facility, Cpl. Hilton dealt with all walks of life. Some of the youth were incarcerated for murder and would be housed at the institution in Columbia until they reached adulthood. Once they were an adult, they would be transferred to another facility.

Cpl. Hilton would conduct his usual rounds in the F wing part of the correctional facility. He would relieve the guard who was assigned to the wing for an hour each evening so that the guard could go on a lunch break. Every time Cpl. Hilton worked in F wing, he always felt very cold and sick. It was only in F wing that this seemed to happen to him.

Cell #14 located at the end of F wing would always keep Cpl. Hilton busy. Every juvenile who stayed in that particular cell would wake up during the middle of the night screaming and banging. When Cpl. Hilton would go and see what was the matter, the youth would say that they were unable to sleep in the cell and requested to be transferred out of there. They would complain that something was pulling on their bed sheets or grabbing their arms. This happened on several occasions with different and unrelated juveniles. Cpl. Hilton had no idea about the history of cell #14 at this point. He would dismiss the claims and direct the youth to go back to sleep.

After telling one youth to quiet down and go back to sleep, he went back to the staff monitoring room and sat down. He was feeling sick again which wasn't unusual when he worked in F wing. However, he became concerned when he thought he was hallucinating. To the right of him, he saw a juvenile offender sitting on the couch watching television. Cpl. Hilton shook his head and looked to his right again, but the juvenile was still there. Cpl. Hilton yelled at the inmate and asked him who had let him out of his cell. Suddenly, Cpl. Hilton watched the juvenile fade away. The first time that this happened, he chalked it up to being some sort of sleep-wake incident. However, he would continue to see the same youth for the next month and half! The apparition usually appeared just before midnight.

With the hallucinations, chills and fatigue Cpl. Hilton was concerned about his health. He was a physically fit correctional officer with no prior health conditions. He made an appointment to see his doctor, but he was deemed to be a young healthy specimen. Cpl. Hilton eventually mentioned what had been happening to him to another staff member. He told his colleague that every time he worked in F wing, he would become light headed and short of breath.

During one of his shifts, he was feeling so ill that when the guard came back from his lunch break, he was quite concerned about the state of Cpl. Hilton. The guard notified the Lieutenant on duty explaining that Cpl. Hilton's mouth was grey, chapped and that he appeared to be very dehydrated. The Lieutenant pulled Cpl. Hilton aside and spoke with him. Cpl. Hilton told the Lieutenant that he didn't know what was going on with him, but that every time he worked F wing, he became very ill.

The Lieutenant asked Cpl. Hilton if he had seen a white juvenile offender roaming outside of his cell. Cpl. Hilton confirmed that he had and said that he must be having some sleep-wake medical issues. The Lieutenant said no, what you are seeing is a ghost.

"A ghost!" exclaimed Cpl. Hilton.

"Two years before you started working here, a kid hung himself inside the cell with his sheets. When the correctional officer's pulled the kid out his cell, he was completely grey," the Lieutenant told him.

This incident occurred on July 13, 2014. A 16 year-old inmate was found hanging in his cell by correctional staff just before midnight. Cpl. Hilton advised that the suicide had occurred in cell #14. The time at which the juvenile was taken out of his cell by correctional staff coincided with the time in which Cpl. Hilton would see him in the staff room. The juvenile was taken to the Lexington Medical Center where he was pronounced dead a short while later. On July 15, 2014 three South Carolina Department of Juvenile Justice employees were suspended pending an investigation into the 16 year-old's death. Cpl. Hilton said that the three employees have since been terminated. It is alleged that they failed to conduct proper arousability checks in a timely fashion which may have prevented his death. Cpl. Hilton was told by his Lieutenant that the young male had been dead for at least eight hours by the time the prison officials had found him. The Lieutenant also told Cpl. Hilton that other staff members have seen the same ghost.

With this new information, Cpl. Hilton began to ponder why the youth had been appearing to him night after night. Cpl. Hilton said that the youth would stare at him with a look of concern on his face. Cpl. Hilton thought it was rather amusing that a prisoner would be concerned about a prison guard. Nonetheless, Cpl. Hilton made his way to the Veteran Affairs Hospital.

He told the doctor that whenever he works in F wing at the correctional institution, he gets weak and depleted of energy. The doctor said his lips were dry and he looked dehydrated. Cpl. Hilton also told the doctor that he had been to a doctor before and they didn't find anything wrong with him. Certainly concerned for his health, the doctor ordered a full battery of medical tests. Cpl. Hilton even underwent a colonoscopy. It was during the colonoscopy, the doctor found polyps growing on the lining of his colon. Polyps can grow into an aggressive and deadly form of cancer if left untreated. The polyps were removed through laser surgery.

Cpl. Hilton often thinks about the young juvenile male who showed concern for him. Cpl. Hilton stated that he was always a fair correctional officer and all of the juveniles liked him. He was even involved in a riot involving 60 prisoners and never had to use any force. Cpl. Hilton told me that if he had never been sent home from work, he probably wouldn't be here today to share his story. He truly believes that the ghost of this young man knew Cpl. Hilton needed medical attention.

Cpl. Hilton continued to work in the institution for several years afterwards, but he never saw the juvenile male ever again. The feelings of fatigue and chills while working in F wing also disappeared after his diagnosis.

Some of the prisoners would still complain that someone or something in cell #14 would pull at their sheets or grab their necks. Cpl. Hilton believes that it is the ghost of the young juvenile. He said that the institution has a high number of African American offenders, and the Caucasian prisoners can often times have a very difficult time integrating into the prison population. Could this be the reason that the juvenile ghost harasses the prisoners housed in cell #14?

PSYCHIC COP II

In *Supernatural Encounters: True Paranormal Accounts from Law Enforcement*, I introduced you to retired Metropolitan Police Detective Constable and psychic Keith (Wright) Charles. After appearing on a podcast, I learned of another police officer with psychical abilities. It is with great pleasure, that I introduce you all to Chuck Bergman.

Officer Bergman is a third generation psychic medium. His mother and grandmother were both mediums. Although it was never spoken about in his family, he quickly learned that he had inherited a special skillset from his lineage. As a child, he could hear voices talking to him on occasion. Every time he would hear a voice or see a ghost, his mother tried to dismiss it as his imagination.

As he grew older, communication with the dead would only occur once every three or four years. The voice in which he would hear, sounded very similar to that of a radio announcer. It was the same rich and pure sounding voice every time. The voice passed along messages with purpose and confidence. The information he received was always very accurate.

Officer Bergman wanted to know if being a psychic was real. There was no better place to find out than Salem, Massachusetts where he grew up. He went to a local psychic shop and paid for a reading. He said that the woman who performed the reading was pretty accurate, especially considering he wouldn't give her any validation. She started out by saying that she saw his mom with her palms open and a little present sitting in her hands.

"Oh, that's nice," he responded.

The day he was having the reading was actually his birthday. His mom presenting him with a present was extremely accurate. They continued the reading and most of the information she had provided to Officer Bergman was accurate. As he was leaving, the psychic told him that she really liked his mom and that if he wanted another reading, he could come back and connect with her again. Officer Bergman thought she was just looking for more money. As he turned toward the exit he rolled his eyes. The psychic then shouted out "Oh and one more thing, I really like your mom's British accent." Officer Bergman stopped dead in his track. Although, his mother lived in Florida, she did have a very strong British accent. It was at this point that Officer Bergman decided to give the psychic some validation. He told that it was his birthday and the gift she saw was in relation to that. This experience was what Officer Bergman had been searching for. He walked away from his reading as a believer in mediumship.

At the time, Officer Bergman didn't realize how much he would appreciate being validated whenever he provided information to someone. It assists him in knowing whether or not the information he is receiving is accurate. As I explained earlier about the dangers of communicating with an Ouija board, the same premise goes for mediums. They are a conduit for the relay of information in which they receive. There is no way of positively identifying exactly who or what is providing that information.

The most chilling message he had ever received involved the disappearance of a two year-old boy. The toddler's mother had gone through a divorce and began dating another man. The man was a local drug dealer and not of good character. Law enforcement suspected that the mother's boyfriend was responsible for the child's disappearance. They had a rough idea on where the body of the toddler may be located. Law enforcement officials invited Officer Bergman to become a part of the search team. As they were searching the area, he heard his internal psychic voice say "You are not supposed to find the body. Go home!"

Officer Bergman knew instantly that he had to honour this request. If he had found the body at the time, law enforcement wouldn't have been able to link the boyfriend to the toddler's murder. Officer Bergman discouraged the search team from looking any further. It was a hot day and the search team had been battling the rough terrain and swarms of insects. He was able to convince them to conclude the search for the day.

As the police investigation continued, they executed a search warrant on the boyfriend's residence. The police located drugs and drug paraphernalia which provided them with the opportunity to arrest and interrogate the boyfriend. While in custody, the boyfriend made a deal with law enforcement. He told the police that if they didn't seek the death penalty, he would show them where the body of the little boy could be found. Police took the boyfriend to the area in which Officer Bergman and the search team had been scouring. The boyfriend pointed to an oil drum floating in a swamp and advised the officers that the body could be located inside the drum. The police were able to recover the body of the toddler and charge the boyfriend with murder. It was this experience which solidified to Officer Bergman that if he hears "the voice", he knows it is going to be accurate and that he better listen to it.

Officer Bergman started his career in law enforcement by serving the United States Navy for four years during the Vietnam War. He was assigned to Special Ops and Radar Operations on the aircraft carriers Shangri-La and John F. Kennedy. After the war, Officer Bergman spent 32 years with the Salem Police Department in Massachusetts. He was assigned to a number of units which included, patrol, motorcycle patrol, information technology, media, and accident reconstruction. He kept his psychical talents concealed from his colleagues during his law enforcement career. It wasn't until he retired that he decided to make his talents public.

Since coming out, Officer Bergman has assisted multiple different law enforcement agencies across the country with their police investigations. He is an author himself and has appeared in print, on podcasts and television networks such as *A&E* and *Biography*. He also conducts readings for the general public. In fact, when I first contacted Officer Bergman, he was preparing for a scheduled reading with a client. He sent me an audio clip from one of his readings to tide me over while I eagerly awaited to speak with him. After listening to the audio clip, I was both amazed and eager to hear more from Officer Bergman. The audio clip was from a reading Officer Bergman had conducted with a State Trooper's wife who was residing in Connecticut. I have transcribed the audio clip below:

Officer Bergman: "Stuff about a clock not working. Is there a broken clock?"

State Trooper's Wife: "Umm… not that I can think of."

Officer Bergman: "He is saying the clock, or it can be a watch. I'll take a watch or a clock."

State Trooper's Wife: "Ryan has his dad's watch and it needs a battery."

Officer Bergman: "Sure, that will work for me because it is the stoppage. But when you look at the watch, just see if it is just a little after 10 o'clock. The best I can pick up on is, it stopped at ten fifteen. Does that mean anything?"

State Trooper's Wife: "Is he showing you that time?"

Officer Bergman: "Yes he is. "

State Trooper's Wife: "His badge number was 1015.

Umm… the watch. I'm looking at the watch right now. (The sound of sniffling). You've got to be kidding me. It says ten fifteen. (The sound of crying)."

Officer Bergman: "He wanted you to look at that. "

State Trooper's Wife: "(Crying) Oh my God."

I asked Officer Bergman to start by sharing his most impressive experience that he can recall. I will now share with you his first story.

After he retired from the Salem Police Department he moved to Florida where he commenced his second career in the field of mediumship. He had a female client scheduled for a reading. As the reading was coming to a close, he couldn't help but think to himself that he could use a drink. Officer Bergman wasn't much of a drinker, but it had been a hectic day for him. The client's parents had come through from the other side and it had been a fairly successful reading. However, during the last few minutes of the reading, his client caught him off guard. She said her sister who lives in Chicago wanted her to ask Officer Bergman about her husband who had been missing for seven days. Officer Bergman concentrated for a moment but felt conflicted about sharing the information he had gleaned from the other side. Her sister's husband had been murdered.

Before making an accusation that someone has died and shattering a person's life, he likes to verify aspects of the information he receives. He started by telling his client that he was hearing a name that started with the letter D. He asked if the name David made any sense to her. His client responded "That's his name, David!"

Officer Bergman then began receiving images of David being at a bank, but he was not cashing a cheque or waiting to see a teller. He was standing behind the glass in the safety deposit box area. Officer Bergman asked his client why David would be roaming around a secure part of the bank. The client responded by saying that David's occupation was president of the bank. Officer Bergman knew he was being recorded and told his client that he was hesitant to tell her anything more, however, he continued. Officer Bergman said that David had been murdered by two men. He could see David lying on his back in very shallow water and there was a bullet hole in his head. The client told Officer Bergman that she didn't know if that information was true or not, because David was still missing.

7 days after the reading, Officer Bergman's client contacted him again. Some hunters had located David's body in very shallow water. David was in fact lying on his back. The police were notified and a forensic team attended the scene. An autopsy was performed, however, the medical examiner had ruled David's death a suicide by drowning. The examiner tried to say that it was a suicide because David still had his cellular phone and wallet which was full of money on his person. Officer Bergman didn't believe that it was a suicide. After 32 years of policing, he didn't understand how someone could lay on their back and drown in three or four inches of water. His client also hadn't mentioned any details about a bullet hole in David's head.

David's wife, Ann, was notified of the discovery. She was an attorney who, in partnership with her long-time retired Federal Bureau of Investigation agent friend, were managing one of the biggest law firms in Chicago. Officer Bergman received a call from the retired FBI agent advising him that they would like to pay him to come out to Chicago to investigate David's case further. Both the retired FBI agent and Ann had heard her sister's recording in which Officer Bergman mentions the bullet wound to David. The medical examiner hadn't mentioned anything about a bullet wound to them.

It was March and Officer Bergman really didn't feel like leaving the warm comfort of the Sunshine State for the Windy City. He didn't directly decline the invitation. Instead, he countered with a ridiculous request thinking that they would turn him down. He advised them that he would require $10,000 cash up front, travel to and from Chicago, lodging, food and any other miscellaneous expenses paid for. To Officer Bergman's surprise, they requested his address and advised that they would overnight a cashiers cheque to him and make his travel and lodging arrangements. Officer Bergman reluctantly agreed.

He travelled to Chicago where he met with Ann. She took Officer Bergman to the scene of the crime. He remembers the location being very picturesque. As they walked toward the crime scene, he told Ann that she must be nervous, because he certainly was. He knew the crime scene had been cleaned up, but he was nervous for the residual energy which may still be present at the pond in which David's body had been found. Officer Bergman told Ann that they weren't alone. Curious, she looked at Officer Bergman inquisitively. He said that there was a female named Elizabeth with them. He could see Elizabeth was pulling off a face peel. Ann said that Elizabeth was her mother who had departed and she always did face peels whether she needed it or not.

As they reached David's final resting place, Officer Bergman walked her through David's final moments. He once again kept seeing a bullet which had struck David in the head. Ann's law firm partner made arrangements with a judge for a second autopsy with a different medical examiner. This wasn't an easy feat. Officer Bergman had to appear before the Judge and discuss his background in law enforcement and his mediumship abilities. The Judge was hesitant to sign the order, but he did. The Judge looked at Officer Bergman and said "Don't make an ass out of me."

The new medical examiner performed the second autopsy and within minutes, he found a bullet wound to the top of David's head. Unbeknownst to Officer Bergman at the time, David had a five million dollar life insurance policy on himself. The caveat to the life insurance was that David could not commit suicide. Where the initial medical examiner had ruled the death a suicide, Ann had been declined the life insurance payment. However, with this new information the death was reclassified as a homicide and the insurance company paid out the five million dollar policy. If Officer Bergman hadn't reluctantly travelled to Chicago, the order for a second autopsy may not have been granted and David would have eventually been cremated. As you can imagine, that would have complicated any future attempt to dispute the suicide.

The initial medical examiner who performed the first autopsy, according to Officer Bergman, was arrested and charged for falsifying his autopsy report. Officer Bergman advised that the criminal investigative team had suspected that there was a connection between David and the Chicago mafia. It was rumored that David had been laundering money for the mob and when he refused to do it any longer, they killed him. Despite Officer Bergman's assistance in advancing this investigation, the Chicago Police Department have not yet made an arrest in David's murder. The homicide case remains unsolved.

THE MISSING SON

Shortly after Officer Bergman retired from the Salem Police Department and moved to Florida, he was contacted by a family from California requesting his help in an ongoing missing person investigation. Law enforcement had been responsible for encouraging the family to seek the assistance of a medium. The family's son had been missing for eight months and all of the leads had run dry. The family wanted to know if their son was dead or alive.

The expression "dead or alive" terrifies Officer Bergman. He really despises the responsibility of telling a family whether or not their loved one is alive or has moved on into spirit form. Although he trusts his spiritual guide who manifests in the form of a radio announcer voice in his head, he always worries about the infamous "what if" scenario. What if the voice is wrong? It is a terrifying responsibility to have bestowed upon oneself. It is for this reason that Officer Bergman tries to verify as much information as possible when he receives messages from "the voice".

Officer Bergman told the family that he would provide them with whatever information he picks up on regarding their son. As he said that, he saw bloody fingers climbing rocks. He described it as if someone had been wearing rubber gloves but had cut all of the finger tips off and just the skin was exposed. He asked the family if their son was a rock climber. His father confirmed to Officer Bergman that his son was in fact an avid rock climber. Unfortunately, the dad's confirmation meant that Officer Bergman was connecting with their son in spirit form.

Officer Bergman looked out of the window in his office toward his backyard. Officer Bergman began seeing big white numbers appear over his swimming pool. They were the numbers 0-2-0. When he was a radar administrator in the Navy, 0-2-0 was a heading. Officer Bergman told the father to take out a map. He asked the dad if his daughter was good at reading maps because her brother was telling him that she was. The dad confirmed that his daughter was very well versed in reading maps. Officer Bergman was on speaker phone, so he guided the daughter to place an "x" on the map where their house was located and then look North 0-2-0 degrees. The family advised that they did it, but it went right off the map. Officer Bergman reiterated that he simply provides the information in which their son was providing to him.

"Dad, does your son own or drive a green Chevrolet

pickup truck?" asked Officer Bergman.

"Yes, and that is missing," the father replied.

Officer Bergman's confidence began to grow with another accurate validation. Officer Bergman saw himself sitting in the son's truck. He described seeing vodka bottles, hamburger wrappers and a filthy windshield. Officer Bergman said that the vehicle appeared to be so disgusting, that he wouldn't drive the vehicle for any amount of money. His dad said that it sounded as though Officer Bergman was sitting in his son's truck, because it always looked like that.

Officer Bergman then began seeing what looked like someone taking a video camera which suddenly tilted toward the dashboard of the pickup truck. He could see the trip odometer. The trip meter was displaying "139". Officer Bergman asked the spirit of the young man if 139 meant miles. The spirit replied to Officer Bergman saying "Make sure it is 139 miles from my house."

Officer Bergman told the family to look at where their house was on the map and go 139 miles north. Officer Bergman said that is where the body of their son and his pickup truck would be located.

Officer Bergman asked if they charted it on the map. They advised that they had. Officer Bergman reminded the family that they had called him and he didn't know anything about their family. He also told them that he was not familiar with California, but if they had put 0-2-0 degrees on the map and went approximately 139 miles north, it should put them near a community with a two part name. The son was telling Officer Bergman that the community's first name starts with an S and the second name of the community starts with an N. The dad responded with "Yeah, that puts him in the Sierra Nevada mountain area."

At this point, Officer Bergman was satisfied with the amount of information which had been validated by the family. He made the decision to tell the family what their son's spirit was telling him. Officer Bergman said that the son had gotten really intoxicated at the Sierra Nevada mountain and wanted to take his own life. The son was going to get married, but his fiancé had an affair with his best friend and he couldn't deal with the hurt any longer. The family thanked Officer Bergman for his time and advised that they would share the information with local law enforcement.

As he hung up the phone, Officer Bergman wanted to throw his cell phone in the trash can and light it on fire. He said he didn't like doing that type of reading and he never wanted to do one like that ever again. Even though everything he had told the family was confirmed to be accurate by them, he still worried that "the voice" was wrong.

At noon the following day, he received a call from a detective with the California State Police. They advised that they were at the Sierra Nevada mountains and had flown a helicopter over where the "x" would have been on the map. The helicopter spotted the pickup truck. Police had to use all-terrain vehicles to get to the location. When the police arrived at the truck, they found the son's body lying next to it.

"Mr. Bergman, have you ever been to California?" the detective asked.

Officer Bergman laughed and said that he has been up and down the Eastern seaboard, but he has never been west of Texas and has never been to California. Officer Bergman explained that he was retired law enforcement himself. The detective was moderately joking with Officer Bergman, but he did tell him that the police had listened to the recorded phone conversation between him and the family. The detective asked Officer Bergman how in the heck he knew where to find the body. The detective said they had promoted the son as a missing person on television, utilized search parties, helicopters, and drones but were unable to locate him or his truck. Officer Bergman explained that it was a gift in which he has been entrusted with, and if he is able to help people with it, than he shall help people with it.

COMATOSE

Officer Bergman's sister Angie had a friend who was involved in a very serious car accident and was comatose for the past five years. Officer Bergman really enjoys working with comatose patients as the information he receives from their spirit comes through even clearer than a deceased person's. Arrangements were made for Officer Bergman to attend the nursing home to try and establish contact with his sister's friend, Katie.

Katie's daughter met Officer Bergman and Angie in the room. Officer Bergman looked at Angie and Katie's daughter and said that Katie was telling him that "Angel is here." Officer Bergman asked what that meant. He no sooner got the words out of his mouth and there was a knock at the patients door. It was Angel, Katie's other daughter. Katie somehow knew that Angel had arrived at the nursing home and was walking down the hallway, but Officer Bergman, Angie and the other daughter were not aware that Angel was there.

Officer Bergman introduced himself to Angel and explained to her that he was trying to establish a connection with her mom. He told Angel that even though Katie is lying in bed comatose, he is able to communicate with her spirit. He explained that Katie said Angel's seven year-old daughter looks just like grandma. Angel was surprised and said that just this past weekend, they had found an old photo of her mother and everyone present had commented on how similar her daughter and mother looked.

Officer Bergman continued and said that the seven year-old daughter was not the favourite grandchild though. Katie had relayed that Angel's little boy, born on February 19, was her favourite. Angel was surprised and asked Officer Bergman how he knew all of this information. He reiterated that he was in communication with Katie right now. He provided the family with a few more pieces of information, but then something peculiar happened. As if they were bored, the two sisters looked at one another and said "Where do you want to go for lunch?"

Officer Bergman was horrified. Here he was, providing an opportunity of a lifetime by communicating with their comatose mother whom they had not spoken to in five years, and all they were concerned about was getting lunch. Officer Bergman concluded his reading and he and Angie departed the nursing home.

Officer Bergman would later find out that Angel's mother had received a large settlement as a result of her car accident. The nursing home fees were eating up a substantial amount of the settlement money. Unfortunately, the mother's two daughters appeared to only be interested in collecting the remaining settlement money. Officer Bergman said cases like these reinforce the fact that he is more concerned about the world of the living rather than that of the dead.

A COLD APPROACH

One evening, Officer Bergman and his five year-old son were out at a restaurant. They had just finished a beautiful steak dinner together. As Officer Bergman was getting his son situated in the back of his vehicle, a gentleman approached him in the parking lot. It was a dark parking lot and when the gentleman yelled at Officer Bergman to gain his attention. Being a retired police officer, Officer Bergman thought he was about to be robbed.

The gentleman began explaining that he was in the restaurant having dinner with some friends when they made him aware of the fact that Officer Bergman was a psychic medium. The gentleman asked if it was true, and if so, could he communicate with people who crossed over. Officer Bergman confirmed that he did possess such an ability.

The gentleman continued to say that his grandmother had died last month. He explained that he really loved and missed her, and that she was more like a mother to him. He asked if he could get his phone number and set up a session with him. Officer Bergman reached into his wallet and provided him with a business card. As Officer Bergman looked into the man's eyes, he said "I just want you to know that your grandmother feels the same way about you. She wants to connect with you." Officer Bergman then informed the gentleman that his grandmother was trying to show him something.

He placed his pointer finger on the left corner of the gentleman's mouth. Officer Bergman then scraped from the corner of the man's mouth all the way back to his left ear. Officer Bergman explained that his grandmother was really sorry that he used to have that scar on his face. The gentleman's eyes opened wide and his jaw dropped.

The gentleman said that one time when he was a little boy, his grandmother had been watching him one afternoon. The gentleman had picked up a fork and began to run with it. He tripped and the fork went into his mouth and cut all along where Officer Bergman had just scrapped. It had left a terrible scar across his face for several years. The gentleman said that his grandmother always felt guilty about that accident.

Officer Bergman said that he wished he could have been a fly on the wall when this man returned to his friends at the restaurant dinner table. Officer Bergman undoubtedly made his evening.

THE GUEST APPEARANCE

During one reading that Officer Bergman conducted, he had two women who were extremely secretive. He can usually see or feel different things about a person's loved one during a reading, but this one was bizarre.

Officer Bergman had a couch near a window in the room in which he was conducting the reading in. The two ladies' mom appeared on the couch. She was providing Officer Bergman with information in which the two women confirmed to be true. Suddenly, he heard a man's voice say "Hey Chuck, tell 'em I'm here!" Officer Bergman looked over toward his couch and as plain as day, the late musician Ray Charles made a guest appearance on the couch next to the mother of his two clients. Ray was wearing sun glasses and had stubble on his face. He was also wearing a white V-neck t-shirt and paisley red boxer shorts.

Officer Bergman was extremely excited but he kept his composure. He wanted to speak to Ray Charles but he was in the middle of his reading. Ray asked Officer Bergman to tell the two women that he was present, but he feared that he would sound like a lunatic. However, Ray was extremely persistent. Lovey was the name of one of the women. She had seen Officer Bergman looking toward his empty sofa, so she asked him if everything was ok. Officer Bergman warned that what he was going to say might sound crazy.

He decided to ease them in by describing their mother. He said that she was present in spirit and was wearing a hat with a vail on the front of it. To the left of her… he hesitated… "I guess she brought with her, her favourite musical artist, Ray Charles." Officer Bergman was expecting the two ladies to say that their mother loved Ray Charles as a musician. However, it turned out that the woman was Ray Charles' mother and the two ladies attending the reading were his sisters.

Officer Bergman had to ask the two ladies what the paisley red boxer shorts were all about. Lovey started to laugh and she said one night there was a knock at the door. Ray had already become really famous at this point and their mother was still alive. Before answering the door, their mother hid Ray in a broom closet. Ray was walking around in his paisley red boxer shorts and a white V-neck t-shirt. There were two rookie police officers who had been attending some sort of disturbance in the neighbourhood. After the mother opened the door, the two officers walked into the house uninvited. After asking a few questions, the closet door flew open. Ray yelled out that he couldn't stay in the closet any longer, it was way too hot. The two officers were star struck when they saw that it was Ray Charles. The family would tell the story many times over the years. Lovey and her sister said that it was a story that not many, except family, were aware of.

When the reading was over, Lovey went out to her vehicle and brought a family photo album to show Officer Bergman. As he flipped through the album, there was a family photo taken with Ray Charles, his mother, Lovey and her sister. Officer Bergman said it was one of his most memorable moments in his mediumship career.

I did find some inconsistencies when researching the background of this particular story. The only sibling I was able to locate for Ray Charles was his brother George Robinson who had drowned before Ray's eyes at the age of four. Ray and his brother were playing outside when George slipped into the laundry tub filled with water and wet clothing. Ray tried to get his brother out of the tub, but he was weighted down with the wet laundry. Ray was only five years old at the time. The other inconsistency was the fact that Ray

Charles' mother Aretha died when he was only 15 years old. This was prior to him becoming famous.

I contacted Officer Bergman to inquire about the inconsistent details that I had found. Officer Bergman advised that Lovey was his sister and the other woman who was present was his stepsister. Officer Bergman told me that he had heard the story about Ray's brother George dying at a young age. Officer Bergman was adamant that the photo album he viewed had mostly black and white photographs of Lovey, the stepsister, Ray Charles and a woman that looked very much like the lady who appeared on his sofa during their reading. He said when he did a little research on the situation himself, he was left scratching his head in wonderment. He suggested that the woman on the sofa may have been a stepmother to Ray.

The only other piece of information Officer Bergman could recall was that the two sisters said they had grown up in a house on West 45th Street in Jacksonville, Florida. Ray Charles was expelled from school for acting out after the death of his mother Aretha. Coincidentally, following his expulsion, he moved into a residence with a family friend in Jacksonville, Florida.

Did the spirit of Ray Charles really come through during Officer Bergman's reading? Earlier we discussed the issue of identity when a medium establishes contact with those from beyond the grave. In this particular case, Officer Bergman didn't simply "hear" the voice of Ray Charles, he also "saw" him. As a parapsychologist, I can't help but wonder if spirits are able to trick mediums into thinking they are communicating with a particular individual, what about the ability to trick a medium into seeing a certain person?

You see, in parapsychology we believe that spirits present themselves to us by using extrasensory perception. They don't have a physical body nor do they have physical senses like we do. They must provide us with perceptions of themselves by utilizing their psi abilities. It is believed that human consciousness is a form of energy which continues to exist after clinical death has occurred. That surviving energy is able to manifest itself in different forms based on how they want to be projected and perceived by us. For instance, if they want to appear younger or older, or if they want to wear a certain article of clothing, they simply picture themselves in that form. If you are one of the lucky individuals who have psi abilities, you will perceive their self-image.

An interesting parapsychological fact is that even an individual who has died under horrible circumstances, a car accident for example, are often reported to look better than they did before they died during reported apparitional experiences. In very rare circumstances has someone reported an apparition looking like they did at the time of their death. It makes sense from a psychological perspective as well. We often think of and present ourselves in our best form and not at our worst.

I'll share with you a personal story which helps puts the parapsychological science into perspective. My dad, Neil Van Dusen had a bleeding disorder called Hemophilia B and he learned in 1994 that he had contracted hepatitis C through tainted blood and blood products as a youth growing up in Ottawa, Ontario. The hepatitis C caused severe fatigue and my father would often need to go for a nap during the day. It wouldn't be uncommon for anyone present or visiting the house to see Neil emerge from the master bedroom and walk down the hallway toward the kitchen to make a cup of coffee after one of his naps. He passed away on August 14th, 2006 due to complications from hepatitis C.

Family friend Lucene MacIntyre was visiting my mother one

time after my father had passed away. Lucene heard footsteps coming from the upstairs hallway and when she turned her head, she saw Neil standing near the master bedroom. She described his appearance as being the same as before he had passed away. Although he was only forty-eight years old, the hepatitis C had ravaged his body and aged him beyond his years.

(Neil Kerr Van Dusen (age 48 and two months before he passed away) with his other son Evan Van Dusen. Photo courtesy of Elliott Van Dusen.)

On another occasion, mom's new husband Ken Farrell had a paranormal encounter with dad in the same Lower Sackville home. While Ken was sitting in the upstairs living room on the couch, he turned his head to look toward the hallway and saw Neil. Ken described him as looking unmistakably younger than he did when he passed away.

(Neil Van Dusen (age 25) with Elliott Van Dusen. Photo courtesy of Elliott Van Dusen.)

Lucene is an old family friend and dad would have nothing special to prove to her. However, he may have perceived Ken to be a threat given that he was living in our family home and was now the new husband to my mother.

There is so much in parapsychology that we have yet to come to understand. Is it possible that the spirit of Ray Charles showed up in Officer Bergman's reading? Sure. It is also possible that another spirit projected himself as Ray Charles as a prank? I believe given our very little understanding of how human consciousness works and our

knowledge of extrasensory perception, that it is certainly possible.

What do you think?

GHOST CHILD

In March 2021, the small town of Mentor, Ohio was buzzing with news of a ghost child. For several weeks, Mentor residents claimed to have been seeing a ghost child wandering their streets. Some residents had claimed to have seen the entity with their own eyes. Furthermore, a small number of residents claimed to have captured the specter on their doorbell and security footage.

On March 10, 2021 at 10:16 p.m., security footage recorded a video of what appears to be a white object, approximately the size of a child, running at a high rate of speed down the road. Upon review of the video surveillance, legs can be seen moving in a consistent fashion as if someone was running.

At 10:40 p.m., the Mentor Police Department received a call from a concerned citizen reporting a seven year old girl running down a street near Bellflower Elementary. A patrol officer responded immediately to the call. This officer witnessed what appeared to be a small child running at an extremely high rate of speed near Wyatt's Greenhouse. The officer exited their patrol vehicle to confront the child, however, the child had disappeared.

The officer searched a nearby building expecting to find the child hiding and scared, however, no one was ever located. The police department even utilized the assistance of a drone and their K-9 unit to no avail.

The officer reviewed the video surveillance from their patrol car, however, the entity was nowhere to be seen on the recording. The incident left the officer baffled as they had seen the entity running themselves which should have been recorded on the in-car video system.

The majority consensus from those who viewed the civilian video footage is that it's a real person running down the road. I applaud the critical thinking skills used in an attempt to solve this mystery. Although, why the police dash camera video didn't record the runner despite the police officer witnessing it still remains unexplained.

THE OLD POLICE STATION

(The Old Police Station situated at 80 Lark Lane, Liverpool, UK. Photo courtesy of Phil Nash and utilized under the creative common licencing agreement.)

The metropolitan borough of Liverpool is home to one of England's most haunted but defunct police stations. The Old Police Station can be located at 80 Lark Lane, Aigburth, Liverpool. It is now a tourist destination hosting ghost tours, market stalls and monthly craft fairs.

The police station is infamous for housing Florence Maybrick. Florence was the wife of cotton-broker James Maybrick who happened to be one of many individuals accused of being infamous serial killer "Jack the Ripper". Florence was convicted of poisoning him with arsenic in 1889. Some believe she was innocent, but nonetheless, she was held at the Old Police Station during her trial.

The cell which housed her still exists today inside the old station. It houses historic police memorabilia.

Apparitions, dark shadow figures, electronic voice phenomena, and poltergeist activity have all been reported at the Old Police Station. There is even said to be an apparition of a former police officer who roams the corridors of the station.

It is not surprising that people have reported haunting characteristics in a historic building like the Old Police Station. Historic buildings such as prisons, police jail cells, psychiatric facilities and hospitals are all structures which have historically had tragic and inhumane incidents occur within the compounds of their four walls. It is entirely plausible that the residual energy from these misjustices remain present in the environment which in turn causes one to experience haunting characteristics.

There are certain common characteristics of a haunting which have been observed, researched and documented by parapsychologists and paranormal investigators for the past two centuries. One single characteristic alone doesn't equate to a location being haunted. These characteristics only become relevant once ordinary causes have been eliminated.

Auditory experiences that mimic human activity are often reported. Reported sounds include; knocking, doors locking and unlocking, laughing, names of the occupants being called, conversations being heard, banging, furniture being dragged, footsteps, glass breaking, doors, windows and cabinets opening and closing and doorknobs turning.

Olfactory experiences such as the distinct smell of aftershave, perfume, flowers, cigar or cigarette smoke, bread or baking smells are frequently reported. Unpleasant olfactory smells are associated to an evil or demonic spirit and include sulfurous odors, rotten meat, decomposition and raw sewer smells.

Touch experiences include the feelings of a hand touching you, being pushed, rubbed, slapped, punched, scratched, bitten and hair being pulled. Another sense known as thermoception which is the ability to detect a change in temperature is also often reported. Cold or hot spots are often felt but may not necessarily be recorded on instruments during a haunting field investigation.

In 2012, a paranormal investigative team heard unexplainable footsteps on the rear staircase. Team members also observed a heavy door open and close on its own accord. If you are lucky enough to be in the Liverpool area in October, multiple paranormal investigative teams offer an opportunity to purchase a ticket and accompany them on a "ghost hunting" adventure. Would you be brave enough to endure an overnight investigation at this haunted location?

THE 6ᵗʰ PRECINCT

Our next story takes us back across the pond to Detroit, Michigan where we will explore another haunted police station. The former 6th Precinct of the Detroit Police Department, also referred to as McGraw Station, has been deemed one of the most terrifying places by the *Travel Channel*. It is located at 6840 McGraw Street and was in operation for 75 years. The Detroit Police Department first began operating out of the building in March of 1931. It was the most state of the art police station owned by the City of Detroit at that time.

The station ceased operating in 2005. Ed Steele would later purchase the building from the City of Detroit in 2013. Mr. Steele wanted to restore the 26,700 square foot building and open a cloud computing data center. While researching the property, Mr. Steele learned that the 6th precinct had a significant amount of police corruption and unrest during its six decade history.

In 1943, approximately 500 people stormed the precinct and released all of the prisoners being held inside. In 1967, the precinct was shot up which required the assistance of the National Guard to get the situation under control. Local legend states that over a dozen suicides, including at least three police officers, occurred within the four walls of this precinct.

While undergoing renovations, workers would complain to Mr. Steele that they were hearing strange crashing sounds and items being moved around. Other workers reported extreme temperature fluctuations. Some of the workers refused to come back to the worksite. Searching for answers, Mr. Steele contacted some local paranormal investigators to scour the historic building. Two paranormal investigators felt someone grab the back of their legs while they were searching the basement of the precinct. Another member of the team had rocks thrown at him by an unseen force. Investigators also heard whistling while they were examining the cell block area.

When one of the paranormal investigators entered the old evidence room, he could feel a sharp shift in temperature and what he described as a heavy presence. Local lore states some of the police officers who committed suicide, did so in the evidence room of the 6th precinct. After looking around the evidence room for a few moments, the door suddenly slammed shut and locked the paranormal investigator inside. He had to call one of the other investigators to come and open the door for him.

If you ever find yourself in the Motor City, Paranormal Expeditions and City Tour Detroit offer scheduled tours of the 6th precinct. Make sure to bring a cell phone with you. You never know if an upset spirit plans on having you unwillingly stay overnight at one of Detroit's most haunted locations.

THE ABANDONED HOUSE

In November 2018, Deputy Sheriff David Barns was assigned to patrol with a police force in the state of Arkansas. He has since been promoted to a detective on homicide. Det. Barns has come across his fair share of strange calls throughout his policing career. It is to be expected when you police a large bustling municipality. One call that still sends chills throughout Det. Barns entire body is an abandoned house situated deep in the rural woods of his county.

Every so often, dispatch receives a 911 call from a landline registered to the abandoned house. The dispatchers only ever hear white static noise. When they ask if anybody is there, they never get a response. Like many other police departments, policy dictates that officers must attend a location whenever a 911 call is received. The strangest part about this house is that there is no electricity or any telephone lines going to the residence. All of the officers who attend this house report feelings of dread.

The first time Det. Barns had ever been to the house was on November 25, 2018. The trail leading up to the house is gated off to the general public. The abandoned house is situated approximately 200 yards through dense brush and trees. As Det. Barns approached the house, he had strong feelings that he shouldn't be there and that he needed to leave. He considers himself to be a rational investigator but he is open to the idea of the supernatural. He snapped a quick photograph of the residence and made his way back to his patrol car. As he returned to the main roadway, he couldn't help but feel that something was following him.

(The abandoned house. Photo courtesy of Det. David Barns.)

As he sat in his police vehicle, he turned on the alley lights and watched the pathway intensely for a few moments. After he had convinced himself that nothing was following him, he reviewed the photographs he had taken to make sure they were decent quality. His shift was coming to an end, but he planned on using his next nightshift to conduct some further research into this property.

The following evening on November 26, 2018 Det. Barns

returned on shift. In between answering calls for service, he was able to find some history on the abandoned house. It was originally built in 1890 and the first deed was registered with the municipality in 1901. The property has been in possession of the same family since it was first built. The current owners of the property now live out of state, but they used to live on the property. During the late 1800's the rural area was booming due to the local mine, however, as with any mining town when the profits begin dwindling so does the community and economy.

Det. Barns met a psychic medium named Michele on the social media application Reddit. Michele was able to provide him with some spiritual insight into the house. Michele said that she had been in communication with a spirit from the house. The spirit was that of an older man who used to be a farmer. The farmer resided in the house during the 1950's. He remains at the residence in spirit form because he enjoys the seclusion. The farmer had no idea why 911 calls were coming from the house, but he too wished they would stop so that he could be left alone and in peace. The farmer admitted that it was him who made those wandering on the property feel unwanted. The farmer told Michele that Det. Barns could visit the property on the condition that he bring a pack of cigarettes. However, Michele warned that Det. Barns should not overstay his welcome.

Skeptical, Det. Barns asked for more details. Michele described a counter next to a doorway in which the farmer wanted the cigarettes left. Det. Barns was familiar with the counter and the description she had provided was accurate. Michele also mentioned an old convenience store several miles from the house. Det. Barns had not told her which community the house was located in, nor did he provide her with the address. He began believing her and was convinced that she had no way of knowing those specific details.

On December 7, 2018 Det. Barns stopped at the old convenience store which was about 30 minutes from the abandoned house. After purchasing a pack regular Newport cigarettes, he continued making his way toward the abandoned property. He exited his patrol vehicle and made his way down the pathway. He began feeling unwelcome. When he was approximately half way from the abandoned house, he stopped and called out to the farmer. He introduced himself and said that he had brought a package of cigarettes as a sign of good faith. The unwelcoming feelings seemingly disappeared.

(The pack of cigarettes left by Det. Barns. Photo courtesy of Det. David Barns.)

Det. Barns entered the residence and called out to the farmer. He advised the farmer that he was going to leave the cigarettes on the counter. Det. Barns also informed the farmer that he was going to walk around the house and take a few photographs. In the corner of the kitchen, he noticed an old photograph of a woman. The picture was sitting on a shelf by itself.

Also on the kitchen floor was an old telephone lying in a pile of garbage. Det. Barns chuckled to himself about the irony of receiving 911 calls from a disconnected phone. He examined the house for any possible way that the phone could make a 911 call, but he found nothing that could explain it.

He had been inside the residence for approximately 10 minutes. As he walked through the living room, he found a passageway that led behind the main staircase. He turned the corner when he suddenly experienced the feeling of being unwelcome come over him again. Suddenly, he heard three loud and distinct footsteps directly above his head coming from the second-floor landing of the staircase.

(The telephone in the abandoned house can be seen in the middle of the picture. Photo courtesy of Det. David Barns.)

Fearing that he may have overstayed his welcome, he decided to leave the house and head back toward his police vehicle. As he was leaving, he took a photograph of the second story window in hopes of catching something. As he continued walking toward his police vehicle, he came to the realization that it didn't feel like someone was following him, unlike the last time he had been at the residence.

As he reached his police vehicle, he noticed another car was parked beside it. There was an elderly female sitting in the driver's seat. He waved to her and she exited her vehicle. She was a resident of the area and wanted to make sure that everything was ok. Det. Barns told her that he was just checking the property as an extra patrol due to the 911 calls the police department had been receiving. The concerned citizen said that the owners live out of state and that no one is ever up at the property. What she said next peaked Det. Barns curiosity.

The woman told Det. Barns that she had been in the house once before. She began describing the cellar in the back room of the house located behind the stairwell. She had heard a rumor around town that there is a bear that lives in the cellar as some locals have claimed to hear loud sounds coming from inside the house.

Det. Barns returned to the office and began trying to locate the home owners. He eventually found an e-mail address for them and sent them a kind message. He never did hear back from them.

Det. Barns returned to the house for a third time. This visit, he entered the cellar expecting to find a bear, however, all he found were cobwebs and old Pepsi cans. It was nothing more than a shallow root cellar. He didn't hear any footsteps or come across anything supernatural on this visit. He had satisfied his morbid curiosity about what was lurking in the root cellar.

On another occasion, Det. Barns took one of the dispatchers who had answered multiple static 911 calls from the residence on a ride along with him. Det. Barns briefed the dispatcher on everything he had done with respect to the abandoned house thus far. The dispatcher seemed to be enthralled with the house. So much so, that the dispatcher convinced Det. Barns to take him to the property.

It was approximately 3:00 a.m. before Det. Barns and the dispatcher walked up to the house. Det. Barnes showed him the outside of the house, but the dispatcher wanted to see inside as well. Det. Barnes felt a little bit more at ease having someone else with him this time. They entered the residence to take a look around. Det. Barns looked on the counter where he had left the pack of cigarettes. They were still sitting on the counter unopened.

Det. Barns and the dispatcher made their way upstairs to the second level where he had heard the footsteps previously. What they saw was old newspapers scattered all across the floor. There was an old mattress folded over itself in the master bedroom. It almost looked like it was covering something. The dispatcher and Det. Barns flipped the mattress over, but didn't find anything unusual.

At that moment, a loud noise emerged from downstairs. It

sounded as if someone was dragging a large stick across the wall. They looked at each other and could instantly tell that they both heard the noise. They both raced downstairs to take a look, but to their surprise they found absolutely nothing. There was no one else in the home and nothing had been disturbed. It was at this point that the dispatcher and Det. Barns had had enough excitement for one evening.

As they began walking down the path, Det. Barns had the feeling that something was following them again. Before he could mention anything, the dispatcher whipped his head around, as if he too felt something was following them. The dispatcher told Det. Barns that if he had not heard the sounds for himself, he may not have believed the story. The dispatcher felt something malevolent belonged in the house and he did not ever want to step foot in there again. That would also be the last night Det. Barns stepped foot into the residence.

Det. Barns still occasionally drives by the vacant property. The mysterious 911 calls from the abandoned house have since ceased. He spoke one more time to Michele the medium. She had learned that there was a malevolent spirit living in the basement of the residence whom the farmer did not like. According to Michele, the spirit in the basement was responsible for the 911 calls. Unlike the farmer who wanted to remain solitary, the spirit in the basement seemingly enjoyed scaring and harassing anyone who trespasses inside the abandoned house.

THE BROWN HAIRED PRISONER

The police department in which Det. Barns was employed with had a policy where all police candidates must work for a period of time as a jailer in their cell block before becoming a patrol officer. At the age of 20, he commenced working as a jailer before transferring to the patrol division and being sent off to the police academy.

The jail had been built in either the 1960s or 1970s and appeared as though it had never been maintained. The building was quite dilapidated during Det. Barns tenure. It was a small jail containing three housing blocks and could only hold a maximum capacity of 60 inmates.

During his first couple of weeks of training, Det. Barns was assigned to a senior jailer who was responsible for mentoring him in the art of corrections. It wasn't a particularly hard job, Det. Barns found the environment to be very relaxed. Prior to being able to work night shifts, several of the employees had told him a story involving a jailer who had been attacked by something in the control room booth where the guards worked out of.

Allegedly, the jailer was completing paperwork late one evening after all of the inmates were locked down. The jailer had told prison investigators that he kept feeling something brush the back of his neck. After he felt it a few times, he turned around and saw a dark, humanoid figure perched on the shelf behind him. As he stood up, the figure jumped at him. The jailer turned around and ran down the steps and out of the control booth. He kept running until he reached the dispatcher's office. The jailer was unable to speak and in shock which led to an ambulance being called. The incident was captured on the closed circuit television system, but the footage was reportedly taken by management.

Given the fact that he was a rookie and that he hadn't seen the footage himself, he brushed the story off as being a prank. Once his training was complete, Det. Barns was able to work the night shifts by himself. After several weeks of working on his own, he became very comfortable with the operations of the jail. He also developed a good rapport with some of the prisoners. He would play cards or checkers with the lower risk prisoners if they were having trouble sleeping and things were relatively quiet.

As he settled into his own routine, Det. Barns would either watch television on the old TV set in the control booth or try and catch a few minutes of shut eye after all of the prisoners were sound asleep.

Sleeping on shift was acceptable at the time as long as you completed one round of prisoner checks per hour. Det. Barns was attending college during the weekdays, so some of his night shifts were brutally long.

During one of his backshifts, Det. Barns completed his required checks and set an alarm on his mobile phone for 2:00 a.m. He verified that all of the cell doors were secured. After being asleep for approximately 30 minutes, he was woken to the sound of someone pounding on the control plexiglass. He woke up to see one of the other workers standing outside of the control room. He grabbed the keys and asked what was the matter. The employee told him that he had heard screaming coming from one of the blocks.

Det. Barns ran to each cell block and was startled to find every door had been unlocked. He shined his flashlight into each cell to confirm that the prisoners were still present and sleeping. He quietly re-locked the doors. Once he confirmed all of the prisoners were secure and accounted for, he returned to the control tower. Upon inspection of the control panel, he realized that the cell doors must have been unlocked manually.

He chalked the incident up to an electrical malfunction

because the control panel was old and had seen better days. As for the other employee who had heard screaming, it must have been his imagination. As the morning arrived, the prisoners were allowed out of their cell for breakfast. None of them had mentioned anything unusual to Det. Barns.

Several months later, Det. Barns was working another night shift. At approximately 5:00 a.m., he and a co-worker were sitting in the control tower drinking coffee and preparing the morning medications for the prisoners. As Det. Barns finished his paperwork, he caught a glimpse of someone walking around in one of the cell blocks through the control tower window. He was annoyed at the thought that someone had managed to get out of their cell. He looked at the control panel only to find that every cell door was still locked. He looked out of the window again and saw a short man with brown hair and a beard wearing an orange inmate uniform. The prisoner was slowly walking around the block with his head down.

As Det. Barns continued to watch him, the prisoner did a second lap and walked behind a pillar. Oddly enough, the prisoner didn't emerge from behind pillar. Det. Barns opened the control tower door and exited the booth. He stormed into the cell block ready to yell at the prisoner, but when he checked the last known location of the inmate, there was no one there.

Det. Barns checked the cell block and did a head count. He even checked the showers and underneath the common room tables. Every door was secure and all of the prisoners were accounted for. His colleague had confirmed that he too had witnessed the prisoner roaming freely. At breakfast, Det. Barns carefully examined each and every prisoner in an attempt to identify the short man with brown hair and a brown beard. No one came close to matching the description.

After breakfast, Det. Barns mentioned the incident to one of the dispatchers who had worked there for 20 years. The dispatcher pulled out the calendar and pointed to a date. She said "Yep, that's him." Det. Barns had a confused look resting upon his face. The dispatcher said the man Det. Barns had seen matched the description of a man who had hung himself in that particular cell block. The incident occurred several years ago on the exact same day.

The dispatcher said the prisoner had been a "repeat customer" or repeat offender; he behaved unusually following his intake to the prison. He was fighting with the jailers and other inmates, talking nonsense and acting insane. She said later into the night, the prisoner took a bed sheet, wrapped one end around the door of the food slot and the other around his neck before proceeding to lean forward causing him to asphyxiate and die.

The dispatcher reported that ever since that particular prisoner died, strange occurrences had been happening at the jail. The dispatcher laid blame on the deceased prisoner as the spirit who had attacked the jailer in the control room several years back.

Det. Barns encountered a few more strange occurrences during his stint at the jail. He witnessed office chairs spinning on their own, caught a glimpse of someone looking through the control tower window when prisoners were locked in their cells, and observed shadows moving across the walls. During the evenings, inmates would report seeing someone in an orange jump suit walk passed their cell door. A few unfortunate prisoners awoke to a third inmate in their two-man cell watching them as they slept.

Det. Barns would later meet the jailer who had been attacked. After the attack, he had quit his job and went to work for another police agency. He refused to talk about the incident and would become visibly upset whenever his colleagues brought it up.

In this particular instance, Det. Barns saw a prisoner with brown hair and a brown beard wearing an orange jump suit which matched the description of a prisoner who had killed himself. There was nothing to indicate that the ghostly prisoner made any sort of intelligent communication with staff or prisoners. This makes Det. Barns story is an interesting one to me as a parapsychologist.

It almost sounds as if it could be a residual haunting. That is when an apparition replays the same scene over and over again at a specific place much like a hologram or a video recording. The apparition is unaware of its surroundings and does not communicate with anyone present. These apparitions have often times met a violent and untimely death. Whether it is a residual haunting or an intelligent haunting, is a moot point. There is certainly enough evidence, and witnesses, to indicate that the jail is haunted.

DEMONIC POSSESSION

Before joining the police force, Det. Barns had travelled to Las Panitas, Nicaragua as part of a week-long mission. It was the summer of 2008 and he was a young 16 year-old lad at the time. It was his first trip without any family travelling with him. In fact, out of the 30 missionaries who travelled to Nicaragua, Det. Barns only knew a young couple from his church.

Nicaragua was an eye opening experience for Det. Barns. He said the highways were in poor condition, the cities and towns were filled with dilapidating huts and run down businesses, and the livestock looked malnourished. He was relieved to arrive at the mission house.

He quickly became acquainted with the 30 missionaries which included several pastors, a few interpreters, and a cute girl several years older than himself. The group was warned that the communities are full of crime and gang activity and to always stay in groups of no less than three. They were also warned that black magic and witchcraft were common practices among the townsfolk and that practitioners were known to curse individuals whom opposed their belief system.

For the most part, everyone had a great experience and the missionaries were amazing individuals. With that being said, the group couldn't help but feel there was a darkness following them around. The best way that Det. Barns could describe it was that there was an unexplained feeling that something was wrong.

Hurricane Alma was scheduled to make landfall the following day, so the missionaries made their way to a small community to hand out some food to the locals. The missionary bus took them off the main highway down a pot hole filled dirt road. Each turn they made, Det. Barns noticed more and more garbage being piled up on the side of the street. The bus came to a stop when he suddenly realized they were at a landfill. Thinking that they must be lost, he was shocked to see pieces of cardboard moving as people began emerging from the heaps of trash. There were locals living at the landfill in squalor conditions.

It began raining heavy and the roadway was turning into a muddy stream. The food truck arrived behind the missionary bus, but the group leader advised that the weather and road conditions were becoming too poor to carry out their mission. Det. Barns and some of the other missionaries disagreed and wanted to remain handing out food to the locals. They were overruled by the group leader which saddened and angered Det. Barns. He is still haunted by the faces of the locals who watched as the missionary bus turn around and leave without delivering any groceries.

The following evening was Det. Barns last night in Nicaragua. The rain had dissipated and several hundred locals filled the stands of a local baseball stadium for a missionary assembly. The rain had shorted out the sound system, so the preacher had to stand on top of the bus parked at the pitching mound with a megaphone. After the service was completed, the pastor invited everyone to mingle at centerfield.

Det. Barns was speaking to a local woman who had introduced him to her daughter. The daughter was practicing her English with Det. Barns when suddenly a member of the missionary group grabbed him by his shoulder. There was an unsettling urgency in his voice advising that they needed help quickly. Det. Barns excused himself and made his way toward the third base. There was a crowd of people heading in the opposite direction. When the crowd dispersed, Det. Barns saw most of the males from the missionary holding a gentleman down to the ground. He immediately thought that something terrible had happened.

As he approached the gentleman on the ground, the group of missionaries yelled at Det. Barns to grab the man's legs. He hesitantly did so. The young local man had a scrawny build and had a horrible stink emanating from him. The man was screaming at the top of his lungs and violently kicking his legs, with what appeared to be superhuman strength. Det. Barns looked toward the man's face, and to this day wished he hadn't.

His face was contorted to the point that it seemed almost inhuman. His mouth was opened so wide it looked like his jaw was dislocated. His eyes rolled into the back of his head and his head was whipping side to side as he screamed. There were men holding his arms out to the side and the rest of the men formed a semi-circle behind them as they prayed aloud. Det. Barns began to realize that they were holding the man in the form of a crucifix. As he became paralyzed with fear, Det. Barns held the man's ankles together with all of his might.

The group began commanding in the name of Jesus for the demon to leave his body. Det. Barns would have run away if he hadn't frozen in fear. The gentleman began to cease fighting. A lady in the missionary group whom was versed in demonology, demanded to know the demon's name. The man stopped moving altogether, took a deep breath and screamed "We are rage!". He screamed so loud that Det. Barns ears were hurting. The voice sounded demonic and almost as if two people were speaking at once. The woman who had commanded to know the demon's name had a look of concern overcome her. She asked the group to let the man go.

Det. Barns said that the man began contorting in ways he had never seen before. As if his arms and legs were spring-loaded, they snapped hard toward his body as he curled up into a ball and began writhing like a serpent in the grass. Everyone backed up and stopped praying except for the cute girl Det. Barns had a crush on. She continued to pray as tears streamed down her face. The man went completely limp as he lay on the ground face down. He began crawling toward Det. Barns' crush using only his arms. As he got closer, she began praying more intensely but also crying harder. As he slinked across the grass with his head still touching the ground, she began to back away from him.

Det. Barns began running toward the man with anger. As he prepared to kick him in the head, he was grabbed by a couple of missionaries who prevented the assault. The girl stopped praying and the man once again went completely limp.

During the commotion, someone must have called for an ambulance. Paramedics arrived on scene and loaded the unconscious man onto a stretcher. Det. Barns had the sudden realization that he had seen the man before. He was one of the locals who had emerged from the trash laden huts at the landfill.

Once the man was loaded into the ambulance, the missionaries began piling onto the bus. On their way back to the mission house, the woman who was familiar with demonology sat next to him. She began explaining to Det. Barns that there was allegedly a legion of demons inside of him and it was unsafe for a lay person to challenge them. The man did not speak English, according to the preacher whom the man had initially approached. The man fell to the ground in convulsions when the preacher laid his hands upon the man's shoulders.

Det. Barns shared that this was his first encounter with the supernatural. He had considered that the man was simply having a seizure, but after becoming an experienced police officer, he realized that this was something different. Throughout his career, he has witnessed multiple people take seizures. He has helped people suffering from neurological disorders and psychosis. He has even come across a couple of excited delirium cases. He believes that those conditions may explain some of the man's behaviour, but he has not been able to rule out demonic possession completely. Nonetheless, it was a terrifying experience for a young 16 year-old to have witnessed.

With respect to demonic possession, I shall lend some credence to Det. Barns experience. The Nicaraguan man displayed several physical demonic possession characteristics such as convulsions, fits, fainting, facial structure changes, vocal intonation changes, rolling of the eyes, and superhuman strength. The only parapsychological characteristic he displayed was the aversion to the preacher which is a holy symbol. The other parapsychological characteristics that a possessed individual can display include: erased memories, erased personalities, gnosis (possessing knowledge for which one should not know), xenoglossia (speaking languages that one should not know), obsession, suicidal ideation, subjugation, and blasphemous rage.

To his credit, Det. Barns was correct in considering psychological and medical conditions for being the cause of the man's strange behavior. Demonic possession often times mirrors mental illness. Dissociative trans disorder, schizophrenia, dissociative identity disorder, seizures, Tourette's syndrome, and other dissociative disorders can mimic demonic possession. That is why a demonologist or clergy rely on observing the parapsychological characteristics in order to differentiate mental illness from true demonic possession.

According to the Roman Catholic bible, Jesus Christ possessed the powers of exorcism. He would pass this gift on to his apostles and what is now the modern day church. The one aspect of Det. Barns experience that I find fascinating is when the woman demanded to know the demon's name in which it responded "We are rage." It reminds me of Luke chapter 8 verses 26 to 39.

Luke tells the story of when Jesus travelled to Gerasenses and met a man who did not wear clothes or live in a house and was bound by chains and fetters. He was possessed by a demon for a long time which would force him to deserted places. Jesus began casting the unclean spirit out from the man. It is said in Luke 8:30 – "Then Jesus questioned him, saying, 'What is your name?' And he said, 'Legion,' because many demons had entered into him."

Det. Barns experience leaves one to wonder whether the man in Nicaragua was truly possessed by the demonic, or suffering from a psychological and medical disorder. One thing is for certain, the experience was absolutely terrifying.

POSSESSION IN PERU

Former western Arctic RCMP Cpl. Bruce Edwards had shared a third and final story with me. After hearing it, I thought it complimented Det. Barns demonic possession experience harmoniously.

Cpl. Edwards was raised as a Catholic and when he was younger, he served as an altar boy for his local church. He served under a very kind man named Father Wally McMullin.

Years later, Cpl. Edwards sat down with Father Wally and a few friends to catch up on life's events. During their evening discussion, the topic of demons somehow surfaced. One of the women who were present said that she believes in evil, but not necessarily the fact that demons may be among us. Father Wally began sharing his experience with what he believed was a true demonic possession case.

When he was a junior priest, he was working over in Peru on a Catholic mission. He was nestled away in his accommodations for the evening when there was a loud knock at his door. He opened his door and saw a local family standing there. They told Father Wally that they needed his help because they thought their daughter was possessed by a spirit. Father Wally was slightly skeptical, but he got dressed and collected his religious relics, bible and some holy water. After draping his stole around his neck, he departed his residence with the local family.

Father Wally arrived at the family's home. He was led into the daughter's bedroom. When he entered her room, the daughter was lying on her bed in a fit of rage or a state of convulsion. Acknowledging that he was not a trained exorcist, he did what any person of faith would do in such a situation, he prayed.

As each passage was read, whatever was inside the young girl was getting angrier. The girl's body went through such extreme contortions, that at one point she began to levitate off of the bed for a moment.

After several hours of reciting the ritual, Father Wally was able to restore peace and order within the girl and within her family home. Whatever had taken a hold of the young girl had seemingly departed. Her facial features and contorted body returned to normal.

As with the Nicaraguan man who was believed to be possessed, the young girl from Peru displayed some of the same physical demonic possession characteristics. Convulsions, fits, and contortions. She also displayed the parapsychological characteristic of aversion to holy scripture, blasphemous rage, and in this particular case levitation.

When asked if he believes in demonic possession, Cpl. Edwards said "I don't know, but I wouldn't bet against it."

THE COLUMBIAN ENTITY

On August 2, 2021 the mayor of Armenia, Columbia Jose Manual Ríos Morales, made international headlines when he shared a video on his Facebook page of one of his security officer's being attacked by an unknown entity.

The attack occurred at approximately 11:29 p.m. at the mayor's office of Armenia in the Quindio District municipality. The black and white surveillance video which also contains a bright exposure, starts out with the security officer walking down the middle of a corridor. The security officer is suddenly and violently thrown toward the corner of the wall. Signage can be seen crumbling to floor as the security officer slams into it. While lying on the ground, something begins dragging him across the floor. He appears to be defending himself as though something were hitting him and keeping him pinned to the ground. The stunned security officer eventually sits up for a couple of seconds before being pushed back toward the ground. Two other security officers can then be seen running over to help their colleague stand up.

After learning of the incident, mayor Morales was terrified. He called Archbishop Carlos Arturo Quintero to perform a blessing, remove any unwanted entities, and restore peace to his office. Although extremely religious, the mayor is certainly a believer in the supernatural. A picture of Jesus Christ can be seen sitting on an end table in his office.

The mayor's office had apparently operated as a hospital for many years before being converted over to government offices. What have you learned about hospitals on this ride along? That they are full of residual energy! Sure, hospitals have occasional happy incidents like the birth of a child. However, the majority of hospital work involves sickness, despair, dying and death.

I find this case interesting because of the amount of violence directed toward the security guard. Individuals have reported being touched, grabbed or on rare occasion slapped by an unseen force. However, an attack as violent as this one is rare. Most injuries that occur in the supernatural are usually reported in poltergeist cases, not haunting cases. Injuries usually occur when someone has been struck by a flying object, or they have hurt themselves trying to avoid being struck by a flying object. Luckily, nothing further has been reported by mayor Morales since Archbishop Quintero performed his blessing. Let's hope whatever violently attacked the security officer has since moved on.

EPILOGUE

Well partner, our shift has come to an end. I hope you found this supernatural ride along to be not only entertaining, but also informative. I enjoyed writing *Supernatural Encounters: True Paranormal Accounts from Law Enforcement*, but I absolutely loved writing *More Supernatural Encounters from Law Enforcement*. The reason? Readers such as yourself. The positive feedback I received from you provided me with the ambition to continue this literary adventure. Besides the entertainment and educational value, hopefully this book provided you with a temporary escape from the realities of the pandemic.

All of the stories you just read are true, many of which were shared with me, and now you, for the first time. Don't let the brevity of some of the stories fool you. I once again researched each story thoroughly. I spoke with witnesses, recorded interviews, researched historical and modern literature, and contacted government agencies under the Freedom of Information Act.

I am always interested in hearing from anyone who has experienced a paranormal event or may be seeking parapsychological assistance. I welcome you to visit my website for the most recent information about PPRI and myself. If you are a former or current police officer, security officer, member of the military, correctional officer, sheriff, or some other form of law enforcement and want to share your story with me, please contact me. I would love to speak with you about your experience(s). I am non-judgemental and offer anonymity.

I had anticipated releasing a sequel to *Supernatural Encounters: True Paranormal Accounts from Law Enforcement* in a couple of years. However, I was inundated by the brave men and women of law enforcement who were kind enough to share their experiences with me sooner than I had anticipated. Perhaps there will be a trilogy in the near future.

Thank you for your interest in this book. Stay safe and I hope to see you again soon, partner.

PARANORMAL PHENOMENA RESEARCH & INVESTIGATION

Paranormal Phenomena Research & Investigation (PPRI), is a non-profit organization consisting of subject matter experts in the social science discipline of parapsychology, serving both Atlantic Canada and the New England area of the United States. PPRI is dedicated to serving the public by conducting ethical and scientific parapsychological investigations, contributing research to the scientific community, and disseminating fact based educational information.

With over 24 years of experience in this field, we have extensive knowledge, experience and partnerships to draw upon. Investigations remain confidential unless agreed upon by our clients.

PPRI conducts parapsychological research and is presently involved in a long-term phenomenological research design project involving encounters of the supernatural across Canada and the USA.

PPRI believes in providing contemporary and scientific education in a field which still has many frauds and misconceptions. Our experienced investigators are available to speak at conferences, symposiums, through media, podcasts, and any other event.

Website:

http://www.ppri.net

Address:

43 Chera Drive

Head of St. Margarets Bay, Nova Scotia, B3Z-0J1, Canada.

E-mail:

info@ppri.net

BIBLIOGRAPHY

Biography. (2021, January 19). Ray Charles. Biography. Retrieved

from https://www.biography.com/musician/ray-charles

Brown, Amy. (2021, April 6). Ghost hunting events taking place in

Liverpool police station where murderer was held. Liverpool

Echo. Retrieved from

https://www.liverpoolecho.co.uk/whats-on/whats-on-

news/ghost-hunting-events-taking-place-20329292.amp

Canadian Broadcast Corporation. (n.d.). Canadians report seeing

UFOs in the sky at a rate of 3 times a day. CBC. Retrieved

from https://www.cbc.ca/cbcdocspov/features/canadians-

report-seeing-ufos-in-the-sky-at-a-rate-of-3-times-a-day

Canadian UFO Survey. (2020). The 2020 Data. Retrieved from

http://www.canadianuforeport.com/survey/data/2020data.pdf

Curiocity Vancouver. (2020, October 13). This abandoned B.C.

hospital is Canada's most famous filming location. Retrieved

from https://curiocity.com/vancouver/entertainment/this-

abandoned-b-c-hospital-is-canadas-most-famous-filming-

location/

Drinkwater, K. G., Denovan, A., Dagnall, N. (2020). *Lucid dreaming, nightmares, and sleep paralysis : Associations with reality testing deficits and paranormal experience/belief.* Frontiers in Psychology, 11, 1-13. doi :10.3389/fpsyg.2020.00471

Dagnall, N., Drinkwatrer, K., Parker, A., & Clough, P. (2016). Paranormal Experience, belief in the paranormal and anomalous beliefs. Paranthropology : Journal of Anthropological Approaches to the Paranormal, 7(2), 4-15. Retrieved from https://e-space.mmu.ac.uk/550/1/Pages%20from%20paranthropology_vol_7_no_1%20%281%29.pdf

Dalhousie University. (n.d.). Eskasoni First Nation. Retrieved from https://cdn.dal.ca/content/dam/dalhousie/pdf/sites/fishwiks/fishwiks_eskasoniprofile.pdf

Elgueta, A. (2021, August 5). Creepy moment 'poltergeist' slams security guard into a wall and drags hima long the floor in terrifying CCTV footage. Retrieved from www.thesun.co.uk/news/worldnews/15788348/ghost-slams-security-guard-into-wall/amp/

Find a Grave. (2013). May Williams. Retrieved from

https://www.findagrave.com/memorial/86375884/may-

williams

Flaherty, J. (2019 September 1). We visited the old police station on

Lark Lane and this is what we found. Echo. Retrieved from

https://www.liverpoolecho.co.uk/whats-on/shopping/visited-

old-police-station-lark-16842460

Grey, O. (2017, June 5). A haunting at Caledonia Mills : The chilling

case of the Mary Ellen spook farm. The Line Up. Retrieved

from https://the-line-up.com/caledonia-mills-the-mary-ellen-

spook-farm

Huffington Post. (2014, April 3). Riverview Hospital video is

spooky even in day time. Retrieved from

https://www.huffingtonpost.ca/2014/04/03/riverview-

hospital-video-

coquitlam_n_5083620.html?guccounter=1&guce_referrer=a

HR0cHM6Ly93d3cuZ29vZ2xlLmNvbS8&guce_referrer_sig

=AQAAAM-

TC5NzbxyD8m70x4HTDgPhiJIgO_tIX60eGKrM6ndECTOf

is8BglksssGxOHaxQNPIpt2e1uuC9K05X8olXEHXiwhNIA

kGUbd81mFMTcc3-

Xt_ThGyOESHWZfaxQ8mTt9gCGxjPxmTDj-

K7Qr6xnE5e9mORFw9Pq8BuNCb16cV

Irwin, H. J., & Watt, C. A. (2007). *An introduction to parapsychology. (5th ed.).* Jefferson, NC : McFarland & Company Inc. Publishers.

Laanela, M. (2014, December 17). Riverview Hospital : a brief history. Canadian Broadcasting Corporation. Retrieved from https://www.cbc.ca/news/canada/british-columbia/riverview-hospital-a-brief-history-1.2876488

Live About. (n.d.). Theories on how Ouija board games work. Live About. Retrieved from https://www.liveabout.com/ouija-how-does-it-work-2594822

London Free Press. (2013, December 9). $325M lawsuit filed over 'shameful' EMDC conditions. London Free Press. Retrieved from https://lfpress.com/2013/12/09/class-action-suit-launched-by-former-emdc-inmates

MacIntyre, N. C. (1998). The fire-spook of Caledonia Mills. Antigonish, NS. Showdown Publications.

Matter, K. (2021, March 24). The haunting of Lake County ? Mentor residents spot "ghosts" in security and doorbell footage.

WKYC News. Retrieved from

https://www.wkyc.com/mobile/article/news/local/lake-

county/mentor-residents-spot-ghosts-in-doorbell-footage/95-

abdf584e-1c3c-4186-902d-c26e4fc4ab98

Nash Ford Publishing. (2001). Ghosts from Berkshire Places.

Retrieved from

http://www.berkshirehistory.com/legends/ghosts_a.html

Nash, Phil. (2020, May 26). Old police station, Lark Lane.

Wikimedia. Retrieved from

https://commons.wikimedia.org/wiki/File:Old_Police_Statio

n,_Lark_Lane.jpg

Open Bible. (n.d.). What does the Bible say about communicating

with the dead ? OpenBible.Info. Retrieved from

https://www.openbible.info/topics/communicating_with_the_

dead

Persinger, M.A., & Makarec, K. (1986). Temporal epileptic signs

and correlative behaviors displayed by normal populations.

Journal of General Psychology, 114, 179-195.

Pictou – Antigonish Regional Library. (1924). Life and adventures of detective Peter Owen Carroll. Retrieved from

https://www.novastory.ca/digital/collection/picbooks/id/1308

/

Renewing Riverview. (n.d.). The history. BC Housing. Retrieved

from https://www.renewingriverview.com/about-

riverview/history

The Black Vault. (n.d.). Spontaneous Human Combustion. Retrieved

from

https://documents.theblackvault.com/documents/fbifiles/para

normal/shc.pdf

The Coast. (2021 February 1). Remembering Ray Charles'

Northwest Florida roots. Retrieved from

https://thecoastal.com/culture/music/remembering-ray-

charles-northeast-florida-roots/

Toronto & Ontario Ghosts and Hauntings Research Society. (n.d.).

Meaford tank range. Toronto Ontario Ghosts. Retrieved from

https://www.torontoghosts.org/index.php/the-province-of-

ontario/central/298-meaford-tank-range

Van Dusen, E. (2019). Evil in Exeter. La Vergne, TN: Ingram

Content Group LLC.

Van Dusen, E. (2020). Supernatural Encounters: True Paranormal

Accounts from Law Enforcement. La Vergne, TN: Ingram

Content Group LLC.

Walsh, D. (2004). That which survives: The case of the near-death

experience. Halifax, NS.

Warren, J. (2013, November 13). Remembering Riverview's dead.

Tricity News. Retrieved from

https://www.tricitynews.com/local-news/remembering-

riverviews-dead-3009206

WIS News. (2014, July 15). 3 DJJ employees suspended after teen

commits suicide. Retrieved from

https://www.wistv.com/story/26012685/dept-of-juvenile-

justice-investigating-death/

WXYZ. (2020, October 13). Go on a ghost hunt at the historic

Detroit police 6th precinct. Retrieved from

https://www.google.ca/amp/s/www.wxyz.com/news/go-on-a-

ghost-hunt-at-the-historic-detroit-police-6th-

precinct%3f_amp=true

Evil in Exeter was co-authored by Elliott Van Dusen. This non-fiction story documents the terrifying field investigation into something so sinister that it will cause you to reconsider your belief in good and evil.

Ever since she was a little girl, Hayley has been surrounded by ghosts. As she grew older, she began to realize that no matter where she moved or what place she lived in, the spirits would seemingly follow her. Their presence and mischievous behaviour had never been problematic until she began to realize that something more sinister was at work. Unsolicited warnings by psychic mediums, a failed house blessing by a Roman Catholic priest, and a chance meeting with a Canadian police officer who happened to be a paranormal investigator would uncover an evil that would do anything within its supernatural power to have Hayley for itself.

Law enforcement personnel are vested with special powers to ensure that laws are adhered to for the safety and protection of the public. Those special powers come with an elevated expectation of integrity and impartiality. Law enforcement personnel are professional witnesses testifying under oath to only the facts of a case in a court of law. When they are faced with supernatural events which transcend from the laws of nature, they are reluctant to share their paranormal experiences. It defies the logic and reasoning in which they are trained to use.

Author Elliott Van Dusen has researched and collected true supernatural events, many of which you'll be hearing about for the first time. Delve into ghost sightings, hauntings, poltergeists, a ghost ship, a vampire and even a demonic possession. Learn how the indigenous people of Whatì believe the Bushman is responsible for some of the missing people in Canada's boreal forest. Discover credible UFO sightings taken from the real "X-Files" which were retrieved from the Canadian Government's Library and Archives. Come on a ride along and experience the chilling true accounts as told by law enforcement from around the world.

THE AUTHOR

Elliott Van Dusen has been fascinated with both the supernatural and law enforcement since childhood. Elliott graduated from Saint Mary's University with a Bachelor of Arts degree in criminology. He completed 15 years of service with the Royal Canadian Mounted Police, retiring at the rank of Corporal. He spent his policing career specializing in major crimes; homicide, sex crimes, and drug enforcement. He currently serves as the Director of Paranormal Phenomena Research & Investigation.

He has earned a diploma in parapsychology from the Stratford Career Institute, a graduate degree in parapsychology from the American International University and has taken additional parapsychological training from the Nova Scotia Community College, University of Edinburgh's Koestler Parapsychology Unit, Rhine Education Center, the University of Ottawa, the University of Glasgow, and the School of Parapsychology.

Elliott's parapsychological work has been featured on the Discovery Channel, The Global and Mail, The Daily News, The Chronicle Herald, and several podcasts and radio stations.